IAN `

A VICTORIAN RESTING PLACE FOR A GROWING INDUSTRIAL CITY

COVENTRY'S LONDON ROAD CEMETERY

This book in its entirety is dedicated to

Emma.

Pie Historical Press

First published 2015

Pie Historical Press

Printed by BuyMyPrint.
Earlsdon, Coventry, CV5 6GF.

ISBN: 978-0-9934971-0-0

CONTENTS

ACKNOWLEDGEMENTS

A view of London Road Cemetery in the 1860s.

ACKNOWLEDGEMENTS

There are many people to thank for help in writing this book.

Firstly Fran Twyman, who first looked at my research a couple of years ago with a view to proof-read the finished book. Fran has gone over and above my expectations in this role and with her patience and some strict editing has helped me achieve the task of finally getting this book published.
Fran and her husband Dave have also been most helpful in getting the pictures to fit and look right.

Other people to thank are Margaret Hobley, Bill and Val Trahern, who in the early stages of my research encouraged me with ideas as to what books to read for research, also introducing me to some of the stories held within this book.

The team at the Coventry History Centre, whose help and encouragement over the years has spurred me on with my research.
Christine Adams, Rayanne Byatt, Robert Witts and John Hewitson.
Also Archivist Carolyn Ewing.

Lionel Bird, Coventry City FC Historian, who has been a great help with all things regarding Singers FC, and providing pictures of former players.

Coventry Bereavement Services, namely Pauline Sparks, Mandy Skett, Greg Gavin and Brian Tranter.

Coventry Bereavement Services also for allowing me to reproduce the Cemetery at the rear of this book.

Also thanks go to The Wright Family, Audrey Bennett, Joan Lee, David Fry, Doris Pails, Janet Leith, Margaret Rylatt, Geoff Barwick, Roy Garland, Derek Robinson, Pete Walters, Craig Campbell, Alan Charlesworth and Trevor Harkin.

Ray, Kam and all the staff at BuyMyPrint, Westwood Road, Coventry, CV5 6GF.
www.buymyprint.co.uk

Tom Poole at Gigante Computers, Cannon Park, Coventry, CV4 7EH.
www.gigante.co.uk

The Coventry Family History Society for allowing me to reproduce the map of the Cemetery, showing the squares which contain the burial plots. For further information on how to purchase the disc they have produced with burial records relating to London Road Cemetery you can contact them on:- www.covfhs.org

And finally I would like to thank my wife Emma and my daughter Penny who have both been a great support during this project, Emma for just putting up with me reading countless obituaries, and my daughter Penny, for providing certain pictures in this publication.

INTRODUCTION

The purpose of this book is to demonstrate the importance and beauty of the London Road Cemetery in Coventry. The lives of the people buried there are a testimony to the growth of the industrial city around them. This growth started with weavers and ribbon makers, moved on to the watch makers and cycle manufacturers and later progressed to the industrialists who introduced and developed the technology of the motor cycle and motor car.

But it was not only these people of industry who developed the city of Coventry, but others who created its social fabric, including shopkeepers, innkeepers, artisans, artists and even architects. Political figures, including many lord mayors are there, too. Many of their stories are in this book. Some, like Starley, Singer and Gulson are quite well known, but others with interesting personal histories are also featured here.

This book includes the biographies of over 60 people. There is also a map at the rear of this book; this shows the squares of the burial plots. This can be used in conjunction with the disc of burial records available from the Coventry Family History Society. The book is not designed as a guide book, but it can be used in that way, if so desired. It is also a way of finding out more about the people within and the structure and design of the cemetery itself.

Over the past few years I have led many walk and talks around the Cemetery, as a member of the Friends of the London Road Cemetery. The group was first formed in 2007 with the aim of making people aware of something that many people walk and drive past daily, not realising its hidden history and beauty.

At a time when genealogy is becoming more and more popular as an interest, visits to cemeteries appear to be on the increase. I believe that it is important to confirm the positions of headstones and memorials and to record their inscriptions before it is too late. I hope this book plays a part in doing just that.

THE LONDON ROAD CEMETERY
COVENTRY

London Road Cemetery was conceived by Joseph Paxton, who later became MP for Coventry in 1854 and filled this role for ten years. In October 1845, Paxton was invited to design a cemetery by the newly formed Coventry Cemetery Committee. Paxton was then at the top of his profession as a designer of parks, gardens and buildings and it was quite an achievement for the city to acquire the services of such a renowned planner.

At this time, there was a great need for a new area of burial space for Coventry. During the late 18th century, Coventry had expanded greatly and the mortality rate had soared, mainly due to overcrowded living conditions. By the mid-19th century, local parish graveyards were reaching capacity and this naturally included the graveyards of St Michael's Church and Holy Trinity Church in the centre of the city.

The area chosen for the Cemetery was situated on the outskirts of Coventry. The site had been a disused quarry which was once a rich source of sandstone used for building purposes throughout the city. Over the centuries, Coventry had had many sandstone quarries and in previous times they had been a rich source of income for powerful landowners.

When the site in London Road was still in use as a quarry, a windmill stood in the place which we now know as the entrance to the Cemetery and maps of the time show this area to be called 'Prior's Quarry'. The section where the Lodge and Anglican Chapel are now, and the part of the Cemetery surrounding them, was known as Quarry Field. The road now known as Quarryfield Road was once the route of the London Road before its course was changed in 1830. The quarry was said to have been used as a makeshift form of trenches when Charles I's artillery attacked New Gate on the city walls in 1642 during the Civil War.

From the beginning it must be said that this new burial ground was not only designed as a cemetery, but also an arboretum, and a 'gentleman's park' at a time when Coventry did not possess any public parks. The lay-out of the Cemetery illustrates this park-like design with walk ways described as 'promenades'. The aspects of the promenades gave views not only across the Cemetery itself, but also across the valley leading down to the River Sherbourne, and Charterhouse Priory. There are three viewing areas specifically made for the purpose of looking across the cemetery and these areas are now taken up by monuments and memorials. Paxton also cleverly used the features of the old quarry such as small hills and valleys to enhance the landscape.

There were three buildings in the original plan: the Superintendent's Lodge, the Anglican Chapel and the Nonconformist Chapel, sometimes referred to as the Dissenter's Chapel. The two chapels were believed to be designed by George Stokes, Paxton's son-in-law. The buildings from Paxton's design, together with the Jewish Chapel, still remain to this day. This is possibly due to the fact that the area has always been a municipal cemetery, and as such has not fallen into such a state of disrepair that it is an unsafe and unsightly area, unlike many others around the country.

The Cemetery was first opened in 1847 and was at the time called Coventry Cemetery. This is how it appears in many of the funeral reports and obituaries of the period, as it was the only cemetery in Coventry. It is thought to be the country's first municipal cemetery, as most other cemeteries of the Victorian period were built and run by private companies. By the turn of the 19th century it was called the London Road Cemetery because, by then, there were other cemeteries in the city, namely St Paul's and Windmill Lane.

The first registered burial took place in London Road Cemetery in December 1847 but it is possible that unregistered burials took place as early as October of that year and were probably the burials of inmates from the nearby Coventry Workhouse.

The part of the Cemetery designed by Paxton is of an area of 18.7 acres and it holds around 6,500 monuments and headstones. There are many more graves than this, however, as many never had a marker. The area of the present Cemetery is 68.2 acres and this includes what is sometimes called the 'new cemetery' which was opened in 1887. The two parts of the Cemetery are separated by the railway line, which incidentally once marked the municipal boundary of Coventry. There was once a footbridge connecting the two parts but this was removed in the 1980s for safety reasons. The newer section of the Cemetery is interesting in its own right as it contains the mass grave of over 800 civilians who died in the Coventry Blitz of November 1940 and the lesser known raid of April 1941. This book, however, deals solely with the northern section, designed by Joseph Paxton.

© IW.

JOSEPH PAXTON

A short introduction to the designer of Coventry Cemetery, later renamed London Road Cemetery.

Joseph Paxton was born 3rd August 1803, in Milton Bryant, a small Bedfordshire village near the Duke of Bedford's Woburn Estate. Joseph was the seventh son of Bedfordshire farmer William Paxton.

He trained as a gardener on several local estates, and then began work in the Horticultural Society's newly-opened gardens at Chiswick, which were laid out on land leased from the sixth Duke of Devonshire. He was soon appointed foreman of the arboretum in 1824

By 1826, at the age of 23, Paxton was appointed head gardener by the Duke of Devonshire to his Derbyshire residence - Chatsworth. While at Chatsworth he undertook other work designing public parks and gardens around the country, including Princes Park in Liverpool, and Birkenhead Park. His work at Birkenhead was later to influence the design of Central Park, New York. It was at Chatsworth that he met and married Sara Bown, the niece of Mrs. Gregory who ran the kitchen at Chatsworth.

On 9th October 1845, Paxton was invited to provide a design for a cemetery for the newly formed Cemetery Committee in Coventry. Work progressed quite quickly once the plans were approved and by October 1847, Coventry Cemetery was opened as one of the first municipal burial grounds in the country. Paxton was paid £300 for his work; the total cost of the Cemetery was £6000.

Paxton was assisted in his design and construction work by Richard Ashwell, who had been Paxton's assistant gardener at Chatsworth. Richard Ashwell then went on to take the position of first superintendant at the Cemetery and he was appointed on 3rd January 1848, on a salary of £130 p.a., plus the accommodation at the Lodge. Perhaps Paxton would have been pleased that his creation was in the hands of his former protégé. Richard Ashwell went on to design Witton Cemetery in Birmingham, which opened for burials in May 1863. Ashwell seems to have remained in his position at London Road Cemetery until April 1866, when he retired. The position of superintendent was then taken on by Walter Dawson, who also ran a nearby plant nursery.

In May 1851, encouraged by Prince Albert, the first International Exhibition of Arts and Manufactures was hosted by Great Britain. Known as the Great

Exhibition, its full title was The Great Exhibition of the Works of Industry of all Nations. It was housed in the 'The Crystal Palace' in Hyde Park, and was designed by Joseph Paxton. Both the Great Exhibition and the Crystal Palace were a great success. People marvelled at the exhibits on display, and the building that housed them.

Queen Victoria bestowed a knighthood on Paxton in October 1851, in recognition of his achievement in designing such a magnificent structure. Being only a temporary structure in Hyde Park, the Crystal Palace had to be dismantled, and between 1852-54 was rebuilt on a much larger scale at Sydenham, then on the outskirts of London, where it became a popular tourist attraction, surrounded by extravagant gardens. The Crystal Palace survived until November 1936 when it was completely destroyed by fire.

In 1854, at the age of 51, Sir Joseph Paxton was elected Liberal MP for Coventry, and again in 1857. In 1862, Paxton supported the foundation of a new school designed for St Michael's, Coventry. Though not regarded as a good speaker or debater, it is thought he played a useful part on several committees, where his practical experience came into play. Sara his wife did not have the same enthusiasm as her husband for his parliamentary duties or it seems for Coventry itself. She is said to have written of 'the scum of Coventry'. This is probably why she never got involved in canvassing for Joseph! He also advocated better railway connections as a way of boosting the economy. This is no surprise, as Paxton had himself invested heavily in the railways, and it was due to these investments that he became a millionaire. In April 1865, Paxton was invited to stand for re-election as MP for Coventry but declined.

Joseph Paxton died at dawn on 8th June 1865, aged 62 and was buried in the village of Edensor on the Chatsworth estate in the churchyard of St Peter. His grave is quite impressive, positioned in the centre of the churchyard and here he now rests with his wife Sara. Edensor is a pictureque village for which Paxton designed a new layout of streets and housing during the 1840s.

The Paxton Memorial was erected in London Road Cemetery in 1868. This project was championed by amongst other people his local friend John Gulson. Initially it was proposed that a statue was erected but this was dismissed in favour of the Memorial that now stands near the main entrance to the Cemetery. It was designed by architect Joseph Goddard, with the sculptor being Sam Barfield of Leicester. This Gothic memorial is now Grade II listed.

The Paxton Memorial as it looks today. © P.Woolley.

PROSPECT TOWER AND ENTRANCE LODGE

Like all the buildings within the cemetery the Prospect Tower and Entrance Lodge were constructed between 1845 and 1847. They are linked by the entrance screen which incorporates the entrance gates.

The Prospect Tower, like the other features at the entrance is built of sandstone and is a great feature that tells people of the Cemetery's presence. Octagonal in shape, there is some debate concerning its original purpose; however, it is clear that it would have been used as an observation post to view the approaching funeral party. The Cemetery at the time sat on the outskirts of Coventry and the funeral party would have usually come from the direction of the city. It is also thought that the tower when constructed would have given views over the valley reaching down to the River Sherbourne and the Charterhouse area. This is now built over with housing on the Lower Stoke Estate. The tower was restored in the late 1980s. This involved refacing the sandstone walls and renewing the roof. Similar restoration work was carried out on the Arcadian entrance screen.

The Lodge, like the tower, was designed and built at same time as the other architectural features of the cemetery. The Lodge, also like the tower, was designed as a focal point when entering the Cemetery. Paxton was influenced by the Italian architecture that he had first seen while touring Italy in 1832, with his friend and employer the Duke of Devonshire for whom he was head gardener. As well as creating a striking entrance, the Lodge was also designed to provide accommodation for the Cemetery superintendent. The person to hold this position was Mr Ashwell, appointed January 1848. The building has two low-pitched roofs covering the main two-storey accommodation section and an additional three-storey tower. The tower and roof would have originally had clay Roman single lap tiles. Unfortunately, at some time the original tiles were replaced with red concrete ones. In 1859, a floor was fitted in the tower of the Lodge to make an extra bedroom for Mr Ashwell's growing family. Around 1869, an extension to the rear of The Lodge was built, being of a single storey, and used for kitchen space. In May 1889, a clock was installed, with the face on the outer wall of

the Lodge, and the workings on the inside of the office. This special clock was commissioned by the Cemetery Committee, and constructed by local watch and clock maker Samuel Corbett. The remains of the clock face can just be made out today, whilst the workings are in storage at the Herbert Museum and Art Gallery. The two chimney stacks, although still quite a feature, have lost some of their impact with modern replacements substituting a small ribbed gable roof to both chimneys. The entrance porch over the front door, though quite grand in appearance, is now missing its sandstone balustrade which would originally have crowned the top.

Records show that electric light was not installed at The Lodge until October 1914.

The interior of the Lodge was converted into offices many years ago and most of the original interior features were lost at this time. However, the long lease on the building was recently bought by a family with the intention of converting it back into a family home and even reintroducing some original features. At the time of writing, only one of these features seems to have survived: the safe which was situated in the superintendent's office.

© IW.

ENTRANCE TUNNEL AND PROMENADE/TERRACE WALK

About half way along the main outer wall which runs down the London Road side of the Cemetery you come across a bricked up tunnel set back in the wall. This is the original funeral entrance to the Cemetery. The protocol on these occasions was that once the bell had been rung in the Prospect Tower, making the workers aware of the approaching procession, a bier, (a hand drawn cart) would be brought from the Carriage House that is set in the inner part of the wall, and taken to meet the hearse at the entrance tunnel. The hearse, horse-drawn in those days, would stop on the London Road and the coffin would be removed Cemetery. The hearse was not allowed in the Cemetery at the time and it is unclear why this was so. It is possible that there was concern that the overhanging trees might be damaged by the horses and hearse. Alternatively, there may have been concerns over the pathways being spoiled by horse droppings. This was, after all, a place also designed to be used as a park.

By 1871, a mortuary was constructed under the terrace next to the tunnel. This mortuary still exists today. During the Second World War it was combined with the tunnel and converted into a public air raid shelter. It is also said the mortuary was used for its original purpose after the Blitz of November 1940

The view of the bricked up tunnel from the London Road side in more recent times.   ©IW.

Between the tunnel and doors to the Carriage House there are three other features in the wall. Two of these features are pink marble niches dedicated to the Illingworth and Causer families. These refer to the earliest cremations in the Cemetery, and more information on these families can be found elsewhere in the book. The third feature is described as a Columbarium. This is a place to hold the urns and ashes of the dead. This one is dedicated to members of the Faulconbridge family. The pathway that runs along this wall makes a pleasant, and in the summer months, shaded place to walk.

The upper part of the promenade also known as the terrace has two rounded towers integral to the wall and a central square tower. All three were originally designed as viewing platforms to take in the vista across the cemetery. Each space would have contained a bench. Originally there was a balustrade here, but this has sadly been lost over the years. A few remaining pieces of the balustrade can be seen on the lower path.

All three areas are now taken up by three very diverse memorials. The first is a Portland stone Cross of Sacrifice, a memorial of the Great War. The inscription reads:-

'TO THE
HONOURED MEMORY
OF THOSE SAILORS
AND SOLDIERS WHO
GAVE THEIR LIVES
FOR THEIR COUNTRY
IN THE GREAT WAR
1914 1918 AND WHO
LIE BURIED IN
THIS CEMETERY.'

During the September of 2014, a full restoration was undertaken by two stone masons from the Commonwealth War Graves Commission. Firstly the whole memorial was cleaned and some chipped pieces at the base replaced. The lettering was re-cut so that the inscription could be clearly read. The bronze sword had been damaged the previous year when someone had tried to steal it. As it could not be repaired satisfactorily it was replaced with a resin replica. This fits in quite well with the patina, giving the same appearance as bronze, but making it totally worthless to metal thieves.

The second memorial is dedicated to workers from the Triumph and Gloria Works who lost their lives in the First World War. There are 66 names in total and the main inscription reads:-

> 'ERECTED IN THE MEMORY OF
> OUR COMRADES WHO
> GAVE THEIR LIVES FOR
> LIBERTY IN THE GREAT WAR
> 1914-1918
> BY THE STAFF AND
> EMPLOYEES OF THE
> TRIUMPH AND GLORIA
> COMPANIES.'

> 'HE WAS A MAN AND NOTHING
> THAT AFFECTED THE
> HUMAN RACE WAS FOREIGN
> TO HIM.'

The Triumph works was based in Priory Street, Coventry, and produced cycles and motor cycles, many of which were for military use. The company had been founded by Siegfried Bettmann, who was also Mayor of Coventry at the outbreak of war. Although classed as a naturalised Briton, Bettmann was the first non-British born person to be Mayor, having been born in Nuremberg Germany in 1863. Bettmann was eventually forced to resign as Mayor in November 1914.

Of the 66 men on this memorial the first fatality was Frank Harris, who was killed in action at Meteren, France 13th October 1914. The last to die was Horace McNight, a turner from the works, who died from his wounds on 11th November, 1918: ironically Armistice Day. The memorial was unveiled by Siegfried Bettmann in March 1921.

The Triumph Gloria Memorial at its unveiling March 1921.

The third memorial on the promenade is for John Heritage-Peters, a local artist, he was a Fellow of the Royal Society of Arts and a founder member of the Coventry and Warwickshire Society of Artists, founded in 1912. John was the chairman of the society from 1925 to 1961 and was instrumental in arranging for Coventry to receive a collection of 90 etchings and engravings by Sir Frank Brangwyn, which are now in the Herbert Art Gallery. At the time of his death John had a considerable collection of more than 70 paintings and sculptures that had taken more than 20 years to collect and were displayed in a large gallery at his home on Kenilworth Road. Some of his water colours are kept in the collection of the Herbert Art Gallery; one in particular shows the building of the council house.

John Heritage-Peters founded the Heritage-Peters Advertising Service Ltd, in 1913. Between the First and the Second World Wars the firm had premises in

High Street and would handle advertising for a number of the big motor manufactures in the city. The business was eventually sold in 1958, but continued to trade under the same name. John Heritage-Peters died on the 9th August 1965, aged 71. His funeral took place at Holy Trinity Church on Monday the 16th August.

Also remembered here is Mabelle Heritage-Peters the wife of John, who died on 5th January 1985. When she died she was living at a home for the elderly in Leamington. She left £4000 in her will to Holy Trinity Church, requesting that the money would pay for a stained glass window in memory of herself and her husband. John Heritage-Peters' final wish was that on the death of his wife his estate would go to pay for scholarships at the Royal Academy of Art. The gift of around £4500 was used to help students of drawing, painting and sculpture.

This inscription reads:

'IN LOVING MEMORY OF JOHN HERITAGE-PETERS
VERY DEARLY LOVED HUSBAND OF MABELLE
DIED AUGUST 9TH 1965

AND HIS WIFE MABELLE DIED JANUARY 5TH 1985

COME UNTO ME ALL YE THAT LABOUR AND ARE HEAVY LADEN
AND I WILL GIVE YOU REST.
TAKE MY YOKE UPON YOU AND LEARN OF ME,
FOR I AM MEEK AND LOWLY IN HEART AND YE SHALL FIND REST
UPON YOUR SOULS.'

It is still a pleasure to walk along the promenade in the way it was intended when first built. It must be remembered that Coventry had no public parks at this time. Here, the citizens of Coventry had the opportunity to take the air in their free time. Today, the visitor has to ignore the traffic noise from the London Road, but writing from experience, 6am is a good time to enjoy the peace and quiet!

Carriage House (Bier Store). ©IW.

THE ANGLICAN CHAPEL

The Anglican Chapel is said to be of a Norman style, but there is some debate as to who designed the building, which was built in 1847, at the same time as the Cemetery was laid out.

When Joseph Paxton designed and laid out the Cemetery he had worked with architectural assistant John Robertson and also George Stokes. Even though Paxton was by now a practising architect it is thought that both Robertson and Stokes would have assisted in the Chapel's design. This is not to say that Paxton would not have had some influence in the design. George Stokes incidentally was son-in-law to Paxton, being married to his eldest daughter.

The Chapel has a commanding position at the top of the sandstone hill which was probably formed when the area was used as a sandstone quarry. Externally, the building has a varied roof-line and a tower which is topped by a pyramid-shaped stone roof, carved in such a way to give the appearance of tiles. The Chapel does not appear to be an early Victorian building as they usually favoured the Gothic style. The walls are of red sandstone, whilst the roof has a mixed pattern of rectangular and scalloped plain clay tiles, with arched windows and doorways. The doors are quite striking with the main entrance being flanked by pilasters with a simple pattern. The windows on either side of the Chapel are narrow and round-headed. Above the main door, however, is a rose window which is quite striking for such a small Chapel. The corbels at the eaves are carved into grotesques that continue to the lower section of the tower at the side of the building.

The interior is modest yet traditional, with a striking timber framed roof. The corbels which carry the feet trusses have each been carved individually with a different design. The main doors are heavy and are decorated with ornate iron work and as mentioned earlier, it is possible to see the attractive rose window situated above. At the time of writing, the rose window is in need of restoration and this will be a project for the future.

Even though the Chapel is small, it has such a commanding position and such interesting features that it has the power to impress visitors from whichever way they approach it. The Chapel is still occasionally used for funeral services, but only at the request of the family, when a burial is taking place within the Cemetery.

On Saturday 24th May 2014, a wedding ceremony took place in the Chapel. This was the first time to my knowledge that this has happened. Brett and Matthew Hill are Christian ministers and chose to have a blessing in the Chapel. Having taken a number of funeral services in the Chapel they both thought it a wonderful building for such an occasion.

Winter 2010.   ©IW.

NON-CONFORMIST CHAPEL

Unlike the Anglican Chapel, the Non-conformist Chapel has suffered some more unfortunate events over the years including theft, fire, bomb damage during World War II, vandalism, and fire again. The contract for the chapel's construction was, as with the Anglican Chapel, awarded to George Taylor, for the sum of £1194.

In contrast to the Anglicans in their Chapel, Non-conformists preferred their places of worship to be more austere and classical having an uncluttered interior. This is certainly reflected in the Greek-style architecture of the Chapel.

The exterior has imposing steps with a central ramp added in later years. A semi-circular path would have brought people to the entrance steps from one side and away down the other side. This approach in no longer possible as the land to one side has been used for burials and the other side has been grassed over. The entrance is flanked by two ionic columns and these in turn are flanked by two rectangular columns supporting an entablature and pediment that form the portico. The portico would have originally sheltered the double doors that took people into the main body of the Chapel. There are two side wings that would have originally had flat roofs when first built, and were hidden by a low parapet. It is thought that originally there was to be a plaster frieze in each of these wings but records suggest this never went ahead.

Inside, the space was open and light with plaster finishing and timber panelling that started from the floor to dado level. The ceiling was originally plaster and lath; this was lost through bomb damage during World War II. In 1900, a new floor was laid of red ceramic tiles in a herringbone pattern.

In March 1884, there is a report of a fire in one of the side wings that was being used to store tools and dynamite! Dynamite was occasionally used to blast holes in the stony earth when digging graves. Health and safety was certainly something that didn't worry the Victorians.

In 2006, the worst fate befell the Chapel when youths set fire to it and the roof and timbers were completely destroyed. The panelled interior and floor tiles were all lost for ever. As the nearest water supply in the Cemetery is at the rear of the lodge, the fire services had to battle to get water into the Cemetery from hydrants in Quarryfield Lane, over walls and between gravestones. It was a distressing sight to see the morning after.

For a few of years, the Chapel looked a sorry state: an empty shell, open to the elements, surrounded by temporary fencing. The Chapel had an uncertain future. Eventually, Coventry City Council and English Heritage found the finances to replace the roof and make the building secure. The work on the roof followed the original design, using slate and lead flashing. The main entrance and all the windows were bricked up rendered and paint black, with access through a door in one of the side wings. This was not ideal, but it has kept the building secure and watertight, while it awaits another use and another chapter in its eventful history.

January 2010.   ©IW.

JEWISH BURIAL GROUND AND CHAPEL

When the cemetery was originally laid out no provision was made for members of the Jewish community in Coventry. This was not rectified until April 1863 when the Jewish community requested that they should have a separate cemetery. An area was chosen in the far southern corner of the cemetery, next to the railway bridge. By May 1863, the designs for the walls and gates were approved and by August the following year they were installed along with landscaping to the area.

This area was outside the original boundary of the cemetery, and it is rumoured that some of the early burials took place while the land nearest the bridge was still at that time in the possession of the railway company. There doesn't seem to have been much dispute with the transfer of land ownership especially as burials had already taken place in it.

The Jewish Chapel is thought to have been built between the First and Second World Wars. It is of simple construction of red brick and approximately 3.37 metres by 4.24 metres. Sometimes this building is mistaken for an electricity sub-station by people passing by on the road. Originally having two double doors and two small windows, the Chapel has its own access gate on the London Road. This is where the funeral party would have entered the cemetery and chapel. This practice was abandoned in the 1980s with all funeral parties now travelling along the Promenade.

This is the only part in the whole cemetery that is still open to new burials.

The Jewish Chapel, not looking its best in more recent years.   ©IW.

Postcard of the Cemetery from 1909.   Author's collection.

RESIDENTS WITHIN THE CEMETERY

To myself and many other people, London Road Cemetery contains Coventry's hidden history and since the first burials of 1847, the site has developed into a microcosm of history waiting to be discovered by later generations.

As part of the research for this book, I have read countless obituaries, character sketches, biographies and spoken to many descendants. This has helped to develop the stories of the people buried in the Cemetery, but sometimes information is more difficult to find. Even the lives of prominent local citizens, some of whom became mayor, or some who were important in a particular industry remain elusive. This is certainly the case with some eminent ribbon weavers and watch makers in Coventry. Their stories are still to be told.

At the back of this book, a map has been provided to help the reader find the people who are mentioned here. Each person has a number which corresponds to the map. This is a system used in similar books concerning other cemeteries around the country. Other items such as the chapels and architectural features are also shown on the map.

Whenever possible I have included a picture of the person concerned at the start of each biography. In some cases, photographs of funeral processions and floral tributes have been used, as these were quite commonly used in the newspapers of the day. Photographs of the monuments and headstones have not been used in most cases, partially out of respect to the families of the people mentioned, and also because the poor condition of some of the stones.

The biographies are not intended to be complete life histories of the people buried in the Cemetery, but instead give an outline of their lives and the part they played in the history of Coventry.

WILLIAM ANDREWS

William Andrews was a native of Coventry born 17th March 1835. His father came from Scotland, and first came to Coventry attached to a regiment that was stationed at the Coventry Barracks. When his term of service expired he was to settle here with a business in Fleet Street where the family lived. William went to school till he was 13 years of age, and then served an apprenticeship with W.H. and C. Bray ribbon manufacturers. By 1852, he was promoted to manager in the design department, and in a few short years he won 14 medals for this, which included a National Silver Medal.

He studied at the School of Art in Coventry, which at that time was held in a small room in the Burges. By 1855, he was artist in textiles at J. and J. Cash, another ribbon manufacturer in the City.

Following the collapse of the ribbon trade in 1860, William travelled to the Continent, working in Paris, and also being engaged as an artist in textile fabrics with a Swiss firm.

When William returned to Coventry towards the end of 1861, he said that he felt a stranger in his own town, as his ideas and habits had changed so much. At that time the ribbon trade in Coventry was said to be at its lowest point in its history.

By January of 1862, he had found work again with Cash's as a designer for £100 a year. William apparently got on well with John Cash but not his brother Joseph. Later in 1862, William became manager of the Kingfield site for the firm but this appears to have not been a particularly happy time as he was reluctant to take up the position. It also appears he was not popular with the workers as it is said he had 'a rather gruff manner about him'. In his diaries of the time at the end of January 1862, it is said that William and Joseph Cash argued. The result of this fall out was William being given a month's notice.

William later went on to work for Dalton and Barton, another well known ribbon company of Coventry at the time. By about 1868, he was in partnership with a Mr T. Burbidge and this lasted till 1874.

William's public career began in 1876 when he became a member of the Coventry Chamber of Commerce. Within nine months he was appointed vice-president, and filled the position of president in 1878 and 1879. William entered the City Council in 1877, representing Gosford Street Ward. He was re-elected in 1878, and not opposed at the three elections in 1881, 1884, and 1887.

William was a prolific writer on the subject of geology, and his writings were published in leaflets, amounting to 30 in all. These included subjects as diverse as history, geology, archaeology and the natural phenomena.

In 1969, the diary of William Andrews was published under the title of 'Master and Artisan in Victorian England'. This book was in two parts, the first taken up with the unpublished diary of William Andrews, and the second being that of the autobiography of Joseph Gutteridge, a contemporary of William's, working in the same industry. The diaries covered the period 1850 to 1866, which is a very important time in Coventry and in the ribbon industry as a whole. It gives a marvellous insight into life in the Victorian era, in a struggling industrial town.

Alderman William Andrews JP died at about 8:40 am on 14th May 1914 at his home 'Steeplecroft', Davenport Road. He was 79 years of age and he had never married.

William's headstone is of simple design and inscription made from slate with a small 'footer' at the opposite end, which is inscribed with William's initials and year of death. Footer stones are more commonly seen in older graveyards and cemeteries, and were used to mark the grave plot boundary. Also interred with William is his sister Ann Carter, who with her daughter lived with him at 'Steeplecroft'. Ann and her daughter had lived with William after the breakdown of Ann's very turbulent marriage described in the diaries kept by William at the time. One particular account details the day in March 1863 when Ann's husband George Carter is described as 'mad drunk'. William and his sister saw a magistrate who took out a warrant against him for assault. By September 1863, Ann and her daughter had moved into William's house, which at that time was in Gosford Green. Ann would keep house for him, and later moved with him to 'Steeplecroft' in Dalton Road.

Ann Carter died on 28th October 1920. She was 83 years of age, and was still residing at 'Steeplecroft'. Her name is spelt ANNE on the headstone however, in William's diary it is spelt ANN. **Grave 45 Sq 59.**

REVEREND GEORGE BAINTON

Reverend George Bainton was a minister for 54 years of which 39 were spent as minister of West Orchard Congregational Church, Coventry. He had only retired from this position three years previous to his death on 21ˢᵗ October 1925, at the age of 78.

He was quite a public spirited man and served on the Coventry Board of Guardians, also taking an active part in politics supporting the policy of the Liberals.

Reverend Bainton was a powerful preacher and great orator, who possessed a striking personality.

The last few months of Reverend Bainton's life were spent as a patient at a nursing home in Winchester which is where he passed away peacefully.

The first part of his funeral service was held at West Orchard Church starting at 11 o'clock, where a large congregation attended. The service was said to be of a fitting simplicity and this part of the service was taken by Reverend W. S. Houghton, a colleague of the Reverend Bainton's from Warwickshire Congregational Union. In a finely phrased and impressive address Reverend Houghton "said they had come that morning to convey to his last resting place on earth one who was beloved by many in that church". The second part of the service was taken by Reverend H. Frost, the minister of West Orchard. The interment rites were conducted at the graveside by Reverend W. S. Houghton and Reverend H. Frost.

Also interred here is George's wife Mary who died in May 1922 aged 69. Mary supported her husband in all his endeavors, and was for 34 years a teacher of the Young Women's Class at West Orchard Church, president of the Mothers' Meeting for 31 years, and nearly 20 years in charge of the Church Ladies Working Party. **Grave 38 Sq 96.**

HANNAH BARNES

Hannah Barnes was born in Knightsbridge, London in 1795. That statement is the only thing that sounds quite normal about Hannah's story, as it was actually in a linen shop in Knightsbridge that her birth took place. Her mother was Maria Fitzherbert who was known to be the mistress of the Prince Regent, later to become George IV. After Maria had gone into labour a nurse was sent for, a Mrs Lowe, who was to become Hannah's foster mother.

The Prince Regent and Maria Fitzherbert were said to have had a secret marriage. However, this match could never be recognised legally as Maria was an Irish Catholic and had been married twice before. The heir to the throne would not be allowed such a marriage.

Hannah's early life was spent growing up in London with Mrs Lowe and her husband. It is believed that Hannah met her real parents just once, when she was five years old.

Sometime later, Mrs Lowe's husband left the family and Mrs Lowe fell on hard times. As a result of this, she and Hannah were forced to move to Warwickshire to live with her parents in Bulkington. Hannah, at the age of 14, started work in the ribbon industry in Coventry. It is ironic to think that she was making ribbons for the rich and privileged ladies of London, when perhaps she should have been living among them.

In 1816, at the age of 21, Hannah was engaged to a Samuel Barnes and they married on December 30th. Not long after the marriage, her foster mother visited Hannah and struck her, saying she had married beneath herself.

Hannah and Samuel had ten children, the youngest of whom was called Annie. When Samuel died in 1875, at the grand age of 79, Hannah went to live with her son and his family. However, records show that in January 1883, Hannah was living at the Coventry Workhouse. This was situated in the building which had once been Whitefriars Monastery. Not all people who were admitted to the workhouse had necessarily fallen on hard times, and this seems to be the case with Hannah. The workhouse admission register states that when admitted Hannah is classed as 'ill'. It is thought that she may have suffered from some chronic illness, or even dementia, and her family could no longer look after her. Having to care for an elderly or sick relative would not have been an option for a working family. As it happened, Hannah was only in the workhouse for three weeks before she died at the age of 87.

Most of these details were recorded by Annie, her youngest daughter, after listening to her mother's stories when she was younger, and they were written in a small black and burgundy note book that was passed down through the family over the years. This was the starting point of a TV programme 'So You Think You're Royal?' which was broadcast on Channel 4 in 2006. In the programme, historians studied the stories in the notebook to establish whether or not there was any truth in Hannah's claim to be the illegitimate daughter of George IV.

Hannah and Samuel are buried together in the family grave along with their son who was also called Samuel. He died in 1908, aged 82. Their daughter Sarah Dadley is also buried here. She died in 1896, aged 79. Also mentioned in the burial records for this grave is an Emma Marson who died in 1928, aged 83, however, her name however does not appear on the headstone. It has not yet been established what relation, if any, she is to the family, but it has been suggested she was a niece.

The headstone replicates the note book that Annie kept, black with a burgundy spine. At the top is etched a small crown with "A FAMILY SECRET" inscribed underneath. **Grave 92 Sq 83.**

WALTER BRANDISH Snr

Walter William Brandish was born in 1878 at Foleshill, Coventry. As a boy he worked at the Premier Cycle Factory Coventry. When Walter was barely out of his teens he decided to start his own business opening a small manufacturing company in Atherstone, Warwickshire. Because he was short of capital, this business was not a complete success, and this made him decide to close his small company and go back and work for someone else to earn and save enough money to get started properly.

There then followed a period were Walter worked for the Triumph Company, Priory Street, Coventry, spending most his time working in the cycle department. In his youth, Walter was known as a racing cyclist on a national level.

In about 1906, Walter founded a cycle repair and services depot on Foleshill Road, calling the company: W. Brandish and Sons. Once well established they took premises in the town at Whitefriars Street, and by the early 1920s increased the range to include motor cycles.

Away from the business Walter was made chairman of Coventry City Football Club in 1928.

Walter died in the early hours of 25th October 1935 aged 58, at his home The Grange, Kenilworth Road. Also buried here is Millicent who died on 14th August 1951 aged 73.

WALTER BRANDISH Jnr

Walter's son, also called Walter William worked with his father at W. Brandish and Sons. It was he who pushed forward the idea to sell motor cycles in the early 1920s.

Walter Junior rode seriously in competition, racing Rover and Triumph machines in many major events around the country. In 1923, whilst practising on the Isle of Man for the T.T. of that year, he broke his leg. The spot where this accident happened was subsequently named Brandish Corner. Walter continued riding in motor cycle trials till the mid 1930s.

Throughout this period Walter worked hard at building up the motor cycle and motor car side of the business. They became Vauxhall dealers in 1932, also becoming distributors of Daimler and Lanchester vehicles from the mid 1940s; however they reverted back to being just dealers in Vauxhall by the mid to late 1950s. They also continued to sell cycles and motor cycles through the 1940s, 50s, and 60s. Interestingly, in the early 1950s they were advertising television sets for sale! To most citizens of Coventry, the name Brandish has always been associated with the sale of Vauxhall cars. Today, the firm of Brandish is no longer in the hands of the family but the company still sells Vauxhall cars. This makes them possibly the oldest Vauxhall dealers in the country, and perhaps in the world.

Walter Junior like his father became chairman of Coventry City Football Club in 1935, holding the post till 1965.

In 1970 at the age of 69, Walter was back on the motor cycle track with many other pre-war racers taking part in a Veterans Parade.

Walter Junior died on 1ˢᵗ February 1973 aged 72, at his home Wayside, Stoneleigh Ave. **Grave 31 Sq 74.**

CHARLES BRAY

Charles Bray was a prosperous ribbon manufacturer who had inherited his father Jonathan's business when he died in 1835.

The firm of Smith & Bray was changed to Newsome & Bray when he went into partnership with Mr Jabez Newsome. Charles retired from the ribbon trade fully in 1856, to devote more time to philosophical and literary studies.

Charles along with his wife Caroline or Cara as she was known, are probably best remembered for their connection with a certain Mary Ann Evans, otherwise known as the author George Eliot. Their friendship began when Mary Ann was about 22 years old. The Bray's home, Rosehill in Radford, appears to have been frequently full of house guests: artists, writers and 'free thinkers' who denounced religion. Mary Ann visited them periodically over nine years, and after moving to London she still kept in touch.

Other points of interest about Charles include the fact that in 1846 he bought The Coventry Herald and Observer Newspapers selling them in 1874 to Messrs Iliffe. Charles was a published author of works on subjects such as philosophy, education, and anthropology.

CAROLINE BRAY nee HENNELL

Caroline was born in Hackney in 1814. Like her husband Charles she was a published author. Her books were mainly educational on such subjects as the laws of health, the British Empire, geography and political features of the United Kingdom. Her most successful publication was probably 'Easy Lessons for Schools,' which ran to 7 editions, with 15,000 copies being sold. There was even a French edition of this publication.

In 1874, she established the Coventry Society for the Prevention of Cruelty to Animals, and for 21 years she was honorary secretary. In remembrance of this, a horse water trough, bearing her name was placed in Queen's Road. It is now situated on Greyfriars Green and is used as a very decorative planter. Cara and her sister Sara Hennell were both great friends and influences for Mary Ann Evans (George Eliot).

Charles Bray died on 5th October 1884, aged 73, and Cara died on 21st February 1905, aged 90. Also in this plot and recorded on the headstone is Elinor Mary who died on 1st March 1865, aged 19. It is not certain who this young lady is, as Charles and Cara had no children. **Grave 11 Sq 42.**

SARA HENNELL

Miss Sara Hennell, like her sister and brother-in-law was a published author and had a critical attitude towards Christianity with the publication of five or six books on this subject. Sara was also an accomplished water colourist and some of her work is still on display in the Herbert Art Gallery today.

She and Mary Ann Evans wrote to each other often, even when Mary was living in London and producing her early books, keeping the secret of her writing even from Miss Hennell and the Brays. Amusingly, it has been found that Sara wrote to Mary to ask her if she had read 'Adam Bede' or 'Scenes of a Clerical Life' by the new author George Eliot. Sara is buried next to Charles and Cara. She died on 7th March 1899, aged 86. Unfortunately, her headstone has been in a state of poor repair for a number of years, after it toppled over and broke into two pieces.

Charles Bray had a great secret, which only came to light in 1977, nearly a century after his death. During his marriage to Caroline he had a secret family of six children with another woman!

ADAM BURDESS

Adam Burdess first came to Coventry at the age of 28, from his place of birth, Newcastle-on-Tyne.

Not long after he arrived in the town, he set up business as a watch manufacturer, making a special watch that was suitable for men who worked on the railways.

By 1880, he had started in the cycle trade in Spon Street, for the production of tricycles only, but moving onto safety cycles, running 2 production lines at the same time. This company, called Burdess and Co, produced Sterling Cycles. Burdess took out many patents for improvements that he made on these machines, and also patented a keyless watch that was of a construction like no other on the market on the time.

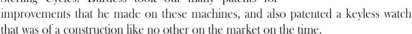

For a few years Adam was a member of the Coventry City Council and represented the Spon Street Ward, being first elected in November 1880 and serving for 3 years.

Adam lived at Dover House, Holyhead Road, and this is where he passed away after a 3 month illness due to heart and liver problems. He died at the age of 68, on 14th August 1892.

Situated at the front of his monument is a large slab with the words 'ENTRANCE TO A. BURDESS FAMILY VAULT.' This slab could be removed at the time of burials to reveal a brick lined vault that would be able to take 10 or more interments. The first name seen on the impressive front of this very imposing monument is Martha Jane Townsend. This is the only daughter of Adam and his wife Martha. She died at the age of 27, on 6th May 1885. Below her name is that of her husband Arthur Townsend who died at the age of 53, on 29th March 1909. Arthur had been made a partner in Adam's watch and cycle business's after Martha had died.

On the left hand side is the inscription for Adam Burdess, and beneath that, his wife Martha Burdess who died at the age of 74, on 2nd March 1899, although by the time of her death she is recorded as living in Edgbaston, Birmingham.

Grave 19 Sq 118.

HARRITT CLARE

Harritt Clare's grave does not have the most striking of headstones in the Cemetery at first glance. In fact, compared to others nearby it is quite simple, being of slate and situated at the rear of the Nonconformist Chapel. But on closer inspection one will notice the top of the headstone has a small piece of white marble set into it on which is inscribed the words 'FIRST INTERMENT'.

Harrit and her husband James ran a family business of boot makers and repairers in Earl Street in the town centre. Before we go any further, by now many people are shouting you've spelt her name wrong! Not so, people have been saying this since the stone was first erected and some investigation was needed. This small piece appeared in the Coventry Herald and Observer on 26th May 1848, written by the stonemason who cut the stone:-

> 'Sir,- I beg through the medium of your paper to correct
> a supposed error which exists in the minds of many
> respectable persons who have visited the Cemetery to see
> the first stone, erected to the memory of Mrs. Clare. They
> think the name is spelt wrong, but I must beg leave to state
> that it is right as she was christened in the Church, and in
> the family Bible of Mr. Clare her name is spelt Harritt, and
> not, as some suppose, Harriet. I had a similar case about
> two years ago, in cutting the name of a female spelt
> Easter, named after Easter Sunday. In this case it was
> supposed I had made a mistake,- I should have put Esther.
> So in this case, her name is not Harriet, but Harritt.
> Yours obediently,
> **WILLIAM SEAGER.'**

William Seager was a well known stone mason in this period and his name appears at the bottom of this headstone and on many others within the Cemetery. However his explanation in the local press didn't correct all misunderstandings, because even in the burial records for the Cemetery Harritt is listed as Harriet.

Harritt Clare died on 12th December 1847, aged 51, and was buried on the 19th December. Harritt's funeral service was conducted by Rev Francis Franklin, the minister from Cow Lane Baptist Chapel. The service itself took place in the Nonconformist Chapel, making it the first funeral service as well the first burial. The inscription under Harritt's name reads:-

'WHILE MOURNING O'ER THIS CLOD WE BEND,
WHICH COVERS ONE THAT WAS AS FRIENDS,
AND FROM HER FACE HER SMILE,

**DIVIDES US FOR A LITTLE WHILE:
JESUS THOU MARKEST THE TEARS WE SHED,
FOR THOU DIDST WEEP OVER LAZARUS DEAD,
O POINT OUR SOULS TO THAT BLEST DAY,
WHEN THOU SHALT WIPE ALL TEARS AWAY'.**

Also buried in this plot is Samuel Clare the son of Harritt and James who died on 21st November 1851, aged 26. James died on 27th May 1861, aged 64, and James's second wife Elizabeth died on 12th March 1881, aged 77.

Records show that when another son of Harritt and James died he was buried in the plot directly on the left of their grave. Daniel Hunt Clare died on 25th February 1889 aged 67. In his obituary in the Coventry Standard he was listed as a shoemaker in Earl Street. It said that he had met with an accident some eight years previously, which is thought to have caused a tumour that attributed to his death. Daniel Clare was said to be a truly philanthropic man, and he had been known to distribute his Sunday dinner to the poor. He was on the Cemetery Committee for around 25 years, which might have something to do with his mother being the first burial. Strangely, there is no headstone or marker on his grave.

A few plots to the right of Harritt's grave is a low grave with a white kerb set and scroll that is inscribed with more names of the Clare family. **Grave 1 Sq 119.**

The slate headstone shows no signs of erosion since 1847.
© IW.

ENOCH CLEMENTS

Enoch Clements was born on 31st May 1841. From July 1878, he held the position of Superintendent and registrar at the Cemeteries, and Superintendent of the City Recreation Grounds. This makes Enoch an interesting character when dealing with the history of the London Road Cemetery.

For many years as well as fulfilling his duties with the Cemetery Enoch was very actively involved with the Coventry Ragged Schools, holding the post of Honorary Secretary for many years. Enoch's name appears in many of the minutes and reports from the period of the mid 1880s till 1895. The Coventry Ragged School was first formed in June 1847 to help educate the poor, as at the time it was said that there were over 4000 children who did not attend school regularly. Later in the history of the Ragged School, John Hough became treasurer for many years along with Thomas Burbridge as Honorary Secretary. By the winter of 1860, the School was operating in a factory premises in New Buildings, and in 1862, a Ragged School for girls was opened in St Nicholas Street. It was from the aforementioned Thomas Burbridge that Enoch took over the role of honorary secretary. During his time with the Ragged School, Enoch became known for his organising skills, particularly in the organisation of the annual bazaar which raised funds for running the school and was held at the Corn Exchange, Hertford Street. This was normally a grand affair opened by the Mayor, with a silver band playing a selection of tunes to create the right atmosphere.

In September 1895, at the quarterly meeting of the Ragged School, Enoch announced his retirement from his role of honorary secretary due to ill health. It was reported that Enoch Clements had shown 'great zeal' in organising events for the school to raise funds. It was also said that teachers and pupils alike were greatly indebted to him, and during the meeting he was given a round of applause in appreciation of his work, after which he was presented with a 'handsome timepiece'. Enoch did not entirely sever links with the school completely as he was superintendent of the girls' school for a few years after.

As mentioned earlier, Enoch Clements was appointed Superintendent of the Cemetery in 1878, taking over from Walter Dawson who had held the role for the previous 12 years. Taking up this position meant that Enoch and his family would have to live in the Lodge at the Cemetery. From this time onwards, the name of Enoch Clements crops up time and again in many reports connected with funeral services and burials at the Cemetery. It is not clear what illness prevented Enoch from continuing his work with the Ragged School, but it seems that his condition also affected his duties at the Cemetery. Gradually, more and more of his duties were taken on by his assistant, W. Cattel, and as a result, the Clements family moved to the nearby address of 20, London Road. Incidentally, on 7th March, 1905, W. Cattel was appointed Superintendent of the Cemetery and Recreation Grounds.

Enoch Clements died on 14th January 1905 aged 63, and it is thought that he was one of the oldest serving council officials at the time.

It is only to be expected that Enoch's funeral would take place in the Cemetery of which he had been superintendent. The Reverend Bainton, minister at West Orchard Chapel where Enoch had previously worshipped, officiated at the funeral. Many councillors and council officials attended, together with staff from the Ragged School. Understandably, the cemetery staff and workers from the recreation grounds department were also in attendance. As the coffin of polished oak was lowered into the grave, resting on top was a wreath in the form of a harp, sent from Ellen, his widow. **Grave 21 Sq 80.**

Remembered with Enoch on the headstone to this grave is his wife Ellen, who died on 7th April 1907, age 59, together with their three sons Ernest, Percy, and Herbert. Part of the inscription on this headstone reads:-

ENOCH CLEMENTS.

SUPERINTENDENT OF COVENTRY CEMETERIES FOR 26 YEARS.

PHILIP COHEN

Philip Cohen was born in Coventry in 1827 and as well as being a highly respected watch manufacturer, he was a prominent member of the Jewish Community. In fact his father Isaac Cohen was the founder member of Coventry Synagogue, and when he died was said to have reached the age of 107 years. Philip was later to hold the presidency of the Coventry Synagogue and it was at this time that the building in Barras Lane was dedicated.

Philip Cohen's watch factory was on the corner of Hearsall Lane and Allesley Old Road and still exists today with a blue Watch-making Heritage Trail plaque on the front of the building. His watches were said to be of superior quality and it was also claimed that every part of all of his watches was made on the premises. This was unusual as many watch makers at this time were assemblers of components sourced from various companies around the city.

Philip was involved in many aspects of public life including the Technical Instruction Committee for the Technical Institute.

When Philip died on 3rd October 1898, aged 72, he had lived in the house and workshop for 24 years. He is buried next to Priscilla his wife who was aged 71 when she died. There are no grave or square references available for the Jewish section.

MARY JANE COOPER

Mary Cooper was the nanny to the 6 children of Edgar Flowers who owned Flowers Brewery. The Flowers family lived in Warwick. When the children had grown up, Mary left the family and at the age of 45, she married Robert Cooper a widower aged 63, who was landlord of the Lamp Tavern in Market Street Coventry.

Robert died in May 1891 aged 73, and Mary took over as landlady. However she didn't like the rough aspect of the job as the Lamp Tavern was in the town centre. By 1896, with the help of the Flowers family, she transferred to the City Arms in Earlsdon.

Mary remained there until she died in August 1921, aged 91. Even today if you speak to some of the older residents in the Earlsdon area, they still refer to the City Arms as Ma Cooper's even though she would have probably died years before they were born.

The grand mock Tudor style building that is the City Arms we see today was built on the site of the earlier one and opened in 1930. **Grave 64 Sq 34.**

Robert Cooper is buried in another part of the Cemetery with his first wife Sara who had died in 1881, aged 62.

The rather formidable looking woman in the white apron is Ma Cooper.

JOHN MILLER DALE

John Miller Dale was one of a group of pioneers that helped form the Coventry and Warwickshire Hospital Fund.

Born in Warwickshire, John began his working life at the age of nine, and he was a lifelong total abstainer. By 1870, John was employed at the Eagle Ironworks Company. At this time he received treatment at the Coventry and Warwickshire Hospital. He was so grateful for the treatment he received, that on the first pay-day after his return to work he stood at the factory gates, cap in hand, to hold a collection from his fellow workers, in aid of the hospital.

John then continued to collect money each week. Wages were paid on a Saturday, which was the end of the working week and so the collection was known as the Hospital Saturday Fund. During that first week John collected 13 shillings and eight pence and by the end of the first year there was a total of £13.

In time, the collections would become regular, and by 1873, the Coventry Working Men's Hospital Saturday Committee was formed. This was the first hospital fund of its type in the country.

Over the next few years the fund steadily increased. £1,000 was reached in 1890, but it would take a further 15 years to reach £2,000. By 1873, the organisation had changed its name to the Coventry and Warwickshire Hospital Saturday Fund. In recognition of its good work, four members of the funds committee were invited to serve on the Board of Governors at the hospital. This was an honour for working men to be allowed on the board as they were normally chosen from the upper classes. As Governors they were issued with 66 tickets each, which enabled them to recommend 264 fund members for treatment at the hospital.

A great number of the medical profession were totally opposed to the fund, understandably worried about their financial standing. They argued that patients who would normally have paid a private fee for medical treatment would join the fund and receive free treatment. The largest increase in both donations and expenditure occurred between 1910 and 1920 and this, of course, included the duration of the First World War. The medical profession's objections to the fund would continue well into the 1930s. In 1931, it was decided to appoint a full time secretary, under the leadership of Leo T March. Subscription rates were standardised and set at men 3d per week, women 2d per week, and juniors 1d per week.

One of John's proudest moments was in March 1938, when he opened the Saturday Fund's new central buildings and ambulance station in Swanswell Terrace.

When John retired he was the foundry foreman for Matterson, Huxley, and Watson.

John Dale died on the 4th January 1940, at his home, 28 Stoneleigh Road Kenilworth, aged 96.

It had been 70 years since John had helped form the Hospital Saturday Fund, and he was still attending meetings shortly before his death. He is buried here with his first wife Catherine, who died 11th April 1889, aged 42, and his second wife Eliza, who died, 30th October 1938, aged 84.

In March 1966, the new headquarters for the Hospital Saturday Fund was opened in Cook Street Coventry. Next to the historic Cook Street Gate, it had been named Dale buildings. The foundation stone was laid two years earlier on17[th] October 1964, by John's grandson Norman Charles Dale. These offices are now the home to BUPA, which now represents people who would have benefited from the Hospital Saturday Fund. **Grave 6 Sq 88.**

The coffin of John Miller Dale is carried into the Anglican Chapel.

ROBERT ARNOLD DALTON

Robert Dalton was connected with the ribbon trade his whole working life and it was as a manufacturer he was most successful. Robert served an apprenticeship with Messrs Sergeants, an old Coventry weaving firm, and later set up his own business. Robert put all his energy into making his business a success as this was a period when many faced ruin because of the French treaty that allowed cheap imported ribbon to flood the English market in the early 1860s. Because of his forward thinking, Robert made preparations for what he could see was about to happen in his trade, when others thought things could not get as desperate as they actually did.

Robert was well thought of in the city by the weavers and members of other trades and on many occasions he would come forward on their behalf to air grievances, spending his own time and money to help them. He introduced the making of furniture trimmings to ease the impact on the ribbon trade, making use of idle looms and skills. He also introduced the making of elastic webbing for use in the shoe trade. The Elastic Inn, in Lower Ford Street is the only reminder of this particular industry in Coventry today. Due to his innovative ideas, both of these industries helped find employment for many workers during what was a most trying time in the history of the city.

Robert built up quite a fortune which at the time was considered colossal. He owned large amounts of land, some of which was sold to make way for Spencer Park in Earlsdon. Dalton Road now creates the boundary that forms the area taken up by the bowling greens within the park.

Robert Dalton was first elected to the Town Council in 1866 for the Whitefriars Ward, was re-elected in 1868, unopposed three years later in 1871, and also in 1874. In 1880, Robert was returned again unopposed and in the same year he was elected an Alderman.

In 1874, Robert was chosen as Mayor succeeding Henry Soden. His year in office was generally a quiet one. He introduced a plan to improve Greyfriars Green, which at the time was an ugly, uneven piece of land on which sheep would graze. This is not a complete surprise, as Robert was by then living at 7, the

Quadrant. This was directly opposite Greyfriars Green and it is most probable that Robert thought he would take advantage of his time as Mayor to make improvements and make it more pleasing to the eye! He also presented the Council with a gold chain of office, which cost £300. Robert was a Council member for 27 years.

In 1869, when his only son Ernest died at the age of 13, he and his wife Sarah presented St Michael's Church, where they regularly worshipped, with a brass pulpit in his memory made by Francis Skidmore. The inscription read--

'To the Glory of God,
And in loving Memory of Ernest Edward,
Their only son,
This Pulpit is erected in this Church, by
Robert Arnold and Sarah Dalton.
Easter Day, 1869'.

In later years, Robert became interested in the growing cycle trade, and became a shareholder in two local companies: the Coventry Machinists Company, and the Hillman, Herbert and Cooper Company.

Robert Dalton JP died aged 68, at three fifteen on the afternoon of Tuesday 10th January 1893, at his residence, 7 The Quadrant. He had been suffering from angina during the weeks leading up to his death. In Robert's will he bequeathed £1,000 in trust to St Michael's Church, part of which was to pay for the upkeep and maintenance of the pulpit he and his wife had donated to the Church. There was also a legacy of £1,000 to the Coventry and Warwickshire Hospital.

While standing at this memorial look down at the stone that covers the entrance to the vault inscribed with 'R. A. DALTON'S VAULT ENTRANCE'. Also interred here are Robert's son Ernest who died in October 1868, aged 13, and Sarah, Robert's wife who died 2nd February 1894, aged 70. If you look a little to the left of this vault you can see a similar looking memorial. This is the grave of Robert's parents: Edward who died in 1851, aged 54 and Mary who died in 1876, aged 76, and his brother also called Edward who died in 1865, aged 44. **Grave 11 Sq 55.**

WILLIAM HENRY FOSTER

William Foster was formerly a sergeant major of the 2ⁿᵈ Volunteer Battalion Royal Warwickshire Regiment. For some years William was the sergeant instructor of the Coventry Companies. He first enlisted in the 68ᵗʰ Regiment in March 1849, and was promoted to colour sergeant by 1850.

By 1851, he had served in Malta, Bericos Bay, Therapia, Constantinople, and also served in the Crimea. This meant he saw action at Alma, Balaclava, Inkermann and was present at the taking of Sebastopol. William also served in New Zealand from 1863 to 1865.

He transferred to the 2ⁿᵈ Warwick Militia in 1866, serving as a colour sergeant for six years. In 1872, he was appointed sergeant instructor to the Coventry Rifle Corps, and by 1881 he was one of the oldest Sergeant Majors serving.

Under army regulations William retired in 1885. He was a member of local philanthropic societies, and was connected with the Hillfields Philanthropic Society.

William died 11ᵗʰ June 1895, at his home 111, Vine Street and he was 66 years of age. His funeral was attended by the local volunteer corps.

Although no personal facts are available, this gentleman certainly had a remarkable military record. **Grave 53 Sq 97.**

REV FRANCIS FRANKLIN

The Reverend Francis Franklin was the first person to officiate at a funeral in London Road Cemetery. He was also minister for Cow Lane Baptist Chapel for 54 years, which was quite an achievement. He was ordained on 11th June, 1799, and as a preacher was said to have great command of the English language and never seemed lost for the most appropriate words. He also had an extensive knowledge of the Scriptures and would often quote long passages from the Bible.

Rev Francis Franklin died on 12th November 1852, aged 80. Rev Franklin's funeral service was performed in Cow Lane Chapel with the Rev Dr. Winslow starting with a reading and a prayer. Rev John Sibree the oldest Dissenting Minister in Coventry at the time gave the address, of which an extract follows:-

'We are about to convey the remains of our departed friend to the Cemetery - the place of sleeping, as the word means. He was the first who officiated at the first open grave in that interesting, melancholy, but lovely spot, and now the grave is there waiting for him, and we are going to perform the same service for him which he performed for so many others. We there shall leave his dust in the custody of death until the Resurrection-day'.

Most of the Dissenting Ministers from Coventry were present and a large number of his friends followed the coffin from the chapel to the Cemetery. Eight close friends and members of his church carried the coffin to the grave. Rev Franklin's wife Rebecca died on 26th September 1855, aged 83 and her funeral service was taken by Rev Sibree, along with Rev Rosevear at Cow Lane Chapel followed by a burial service at the Cemetery.

Francis and Rebecca Franklin had two daughters, Mary and Rebecca and both were very well educated. They set up and ran a small private boarding school for young ladies, known as 'Nant Glyn', in the smartest part of Coventry at the time: Warwick Row. The building still stands today, 29 Warwick Row, and has been occupied for many years by local estate agent, Loveitts. In 1832, a bright 13 year girl called Mary Ann Evans started to attend the school. This young lady would be better known in years to come as writer George Eliot. The curriculum of the school included history and drawing taught by Mary and Rebecca's brother George. Music was also included and as Mary Ann became the best pianist at the school, she was occasionally asked to play for visitors. Rebecca Franklin had spent some time in Paris, in order to improve her French, and this would have been beneficial to Mary Ann's own grasp of the language. Rebecca also taught English and Mary taught arithmetic. Under the influence of the Franklin sisters, Mary Ann was even said to have lost her Midlands accent. As mentioned elsewhere in this book, Mary Ann's time in Coventry was a great influence in her social and academic growth and perhaps contributed to the development of her literary success. The Franklin family may have also inspired some of the characters in her books, as the Reverend Franklin has been identified as the character Reverend Rufus Lyon in the novel 'Felix Holt the Radical' of 1866.

Mary Franklin died in December 1867, aged 67, while Rebecca died six years later in June 1873, aged 69. The grave is positioned to the rear of the Non-Conformist Chapel. The stonework on the grave consists of a large four sided white marble piece and there are many other family names inscribed on it. Records show these names refer to people buried in a larger grave next to this plot. **Grave 4 Sq 119.**

DAVID GEE

David Gee was born in Spon Street on the 24th December 1793. His father was a watchmaker and young David attended Fairfax's School for three years from the age of nine and a half.

While at school he practised drawing, and by the time he was 13 he sold his first painting titled "The Death of Nelson", which was sold for the sum of five shillings.

On leaving school David was apprenticed to his father as a watchmaker. After his apprenticeship he continued in the watch trade, until he was 25 years old. This however was not to be his career. As an artist David was self-taught but he was still confident enough to become a full time painter between about 1818 and 1820.

Around this time Lord Bridport commissioned two paintings of naval battles, which meant David would spend some months living in London where his talents were recognised by the then president of the Royal Academy, Sir Benjamin West. However, David did not like London and as soon as he could he returned to Coventry.

He had many local commissions from wealthy families such as the Hoods and the Gregorys. He also produced armorial bearings for carriages, and public house signs. In around 1830, he began a series of Coventry towns-capes and views of churches.

In June 1851, David's first wife Mary died at the age of 55 and in 1857, when in his mid-sixties, David married again to a local woman named Harriet who was in her late forties. Sadly, she died in April 1868, aged 59. Mary and Harriet are both buried here, David outliving them both, dying in January 1872, aged 78.

The stone that covers this grave is one complete slab lying flat, if you look carefully under David's name inscribed is the word "ARTIST". **Grave 38 Sq 56.**

GEORGE GIBSON

George Gibson served Coventry Education Authority for 49 years, and was a pioneer of the advance classes run in connection with Coventry's elementary schools. He was also instrumental in introducing school gardens to Coventry, making it one of the first urban areas to have school gardens in the country.

After acting as a pupil-teacher at South Street School, Hillfields from 1881 till 1886, George completed his studies at St Mark's Teacher Training College, London, and returned to South Street School in 1889, to become chief assistant.

George found himself teaching a class of 71 boys! The boys were poorly clothed, under-nourished, and in the main, bootless. As a result of this George placed a 'boot box' on his desk inviting visitors and the better-off boys to contribute money to buy boots and clothes for those in need.

George had many influential friends and at a meeting in 1893, presided over by Thomas Burbage, it was recorded that William Hillman, John Gulson, James Starley, Joseph Cash, Dr Webb Fowler, and Rev F. Beaumont all supported the decision to start a fund that would be city-wide.

After a few years he went to Wheatley Street School, and in 1895 was appointed headmaster of the new Red Lane Senior Mixed School. He was here until August 1905 when he took up the headship of the new Frederick Bird Senior Mixed School. He retired as headmaster of Frederick Bird School in 1932.

George Gibson died on 7th February 1938, aged 70. The Coventry Boot Fund is a fitting memorial to a caring teacher and his colleagues, who helped those in need more than a century ago. The Children's Boot Fund is still in existence today, and has served the children of Coventry through the depression of the 1930s, two world wars and the ups and downs of the late 20th century. It is probably just as relevant today as it was over a 100 years ago.

George is interred here with his wife Alice who died on 23rd April 1924, aged 55. **Grave 25 Sq 64.**

ELI GREEN

Born in Gosford Street in 1818 the son of a labourer, Eli Green was to become a master weaver who would make his fortune in the silk trade. When Eli started in the weaving trade, dresses and bonnets were trimmed with fancy ribbons and were at the height of fashion.

Even though he was poorly educated he was able to start his own business at the age of 20. It was at this time he married his childhood sweetheart, Ann Sansome, the daughter of a neighbouring weaver. Sadly, Ann died from TB in 1855, at the age of 39, leaving Eli with three children to raise.

Eli will be best remembered for building a triangle of top shops in Hillfields. Top shops were houses built specially for ribbon weavers and were houses with an extra top storey that was used as a workshop. The top storey was designed with one side made almost completely of windows to provide light from which to work from.

The triangle of top shops was built in 1858 and became very profitable. There were 67 in total, with all the looms being powered by a steam engine that was installed at the corner of Berry Street and Vernon Street. This drove the looms on the second floor, making ribbons that the occupants would then sell to Eli. However, the weaver would still have to pay him rent for the power they used.

Eli became a wealthy man, even owning a quarry and in 1864 he bought a gentleman's house at Foleshill just outside Coventry. It was called Heath House and this is where Eli would live until he died on 9th August 1899, at the age of 81.
Grave 31 Sq 31.

A footnote to this is that Eli's grandson William Bassett-Green became a prosperous estate developer, and the Lady Godiva statue in Broadgate was a gift from him to the City. The statue was unveiled in 1949 and cost £20,000, and was designed by Sir William Reid-Dick.

JOHN GULSON

John Gulson was born in Coventry on 23rd October 1813. He was to play a great part in municipal life within the city. His father was John Gulson senior, who was born in Leicester in 1761, and came to Coventry to serve an apprenticeship in the leather trade, becoming a freeman in 1785. His wife Elizabeth came from a London Quaker family. John and Elizabeth lived at 130 Spon Street, Coventry with their family which consisted of John and three daughters.

In 1837, the family moved to 7, Priory Row, a fine Georgian house which still stands today. The three daughters were Elizabeth, Ann and Rachel. Rachel the youngest died in 1839, aged 23, and was buried in the Quaker Burial Ground in Hill Street. Elizabeth and Ann went on to marry gentlemen from Leicester and this would lead to their parents moving to Leicester in 1847, leaving John in residence at Priory Row.

John's father seems to have withdrawn from public life from around 1835, however John continued with his father's interests, especially in community work. In 1835, John was made joint secretary of the Mechanics Institute along with James Sibley Whittem, at this time manager of Wyken Colliery. During their time in this position, a new Mechanic's Institute was built in Hertford Street, at the top of the street where Lloyds Bank is now situated. It was the pride of the Gulson family. They hoped that Coventry's workers would use it as a centre of learning for adults for the advancement of their education. The family and their friends had raised most of the money needed for the building's construction.

Sir Joseph Paxton, a close friend of John and designer of the Cemetery, once said, "A man who invents new want is a benefactor to society" John would take his friend's advice and would follow the trends in Coventry's trade.

In 1838, John had set up in business going into partnership with a Mr Merrick, a silk broker. The firm was known as Merrick and Gulson and had an office in Vicar Lane. John learnt a great deal about the silk trade from Merrick, in particular the method of buying raw silk in London and then selling it on in Coventry. Merrick eventually left Coventry and moved to Manchester. From that time on, John worked alone and prospered, moving to new offices in High Street.

In politics, John was a Liberal and in 1841 he presented to the Corporation a petition that he had organized, asking it to support the repeal of the Corn Laws. The Corn Laws were trade laws designed to protect cereal producers in the United Kingdom of Great Britain and Ireland against competition from less expensive foreign imports between 1815 and 1846. To ensure that British landowners reaped all the financial profits from farming, the corn laws imposed steep import duties, making it too expensive for anyone to import grain from other countries, even when the people of Great Britain and Ireland needed the food (as in times of famine). John Gulson's public and voluntary service was honoured, and in 1847 he was nominated as an alderman of the City of Coventry. This was not the usual route to being elected, it would normally have been as a representative of one of the wards, but the Town Council had the powers that are in the Municipal Corporations Act of 1835: this is not a well-known power because it is seldom used.

By 1850, John went into partnership with Richard Caldicott and this lasted till 1872, when the partnership was dissolved. From this time onwards John had business connections with the Coventry Machinists Company, the cycle manufacturers, and kept this interest until 1896.

The year 1862 would be one of change in John's life, for on 6th November he married Sophia Louisa Miller, the eldest daughter of John Rowley Miller, of Moneymore, Ireland. The ceremony took place at St John's Church, Moneymore. John and Sophia had much in common: they both had a love for the open air, a great love of gardens, and they were also anxious to help those in need, those less fortunate and the sick.

In 1863, John bought as an investment, the Manor Farm at Stapleton, an East Leicestershire village. As mentioned earlier the Gulsons in Leicestershire were well connected. On purchasing Manor Farm, John became the lord of the manor and the farm was tenanted by a family called Grewcock.

John's second rural property was 'The Spring' at Stoke on the eastern outskirts of Coventry. This was primarily bought as a summer residence for himself and Sophia; this is not as unusual as it may sound, as many wealthy business men had houses built in this area for the summer months. 'The Spring' was demolished in the late 1920s or early 1930s and this area of Lower Stoke is now known as 'Poets Corner,' containing streets such as Keats Road, Lord Lytton Avenue and Meredith Road.

When John's great friend Sir Joseph Paxton, designer of the Cemetery and MP for Coventry from 1854 to 1865, died on 8th June 1865, John suggested that his life should be commemorated in some way. This was not a popular idea with all of Coventry's citizens because he was not always well regarded as an MP. John promoted a fund which was eventually used to pay for the memorial that now stands at the entrance to the Cemetery. It was completed in 1866.

In Sir Joseph's will he made a bequest to John: the sum of nineteen guineas with which to buy a ring or some other token of their friendship. John brought a rain gauge and a pair of binoculars with the money, and for many years afterwards used the gauge for his records of rainfall in Coventry! His first report appeared in the Coventry Standard on 3rd June 1870.

In November 1867, John had the great honour of being elected Mayor of Coventry. By this time he was highly respected as a kind-hearted and philanthropic man who was always ready to help the poor and suffering, and also as 'a public spirited citizen of sound ideas'. During his term as Mayor the distress amongst the weavers was great and John subscribed the sum of £21 to the relief fund. As well as assisting the Technical Education movement, he also promoted physical development in young men, patronising the Gymnasium and Athletic Club and distributing the prizes in 1868.

Perhaps his greatest achievement as Mayor was the founding of the Free Library in Hertford Street. John believed that there should be a free reading service in the city and when he opened the library in 1868, 17,000 volumes were made available to the citizens of Coventry. He was pleased with his achievement but felt that more should be done to help the people. In the 1870s, John bought the site of the Old Gaol and presented it to the city for the purpose of building a permanent library. Cathedral Lanes now stands on the site of the library.

December 22nd 1895 would have been one of John's saddest days, as this is when his wife Sophia died at the age of 63. She had supported John in all his endeavours, and was greatly mourned by the city. Sophia had been involved in the setting up of children's wards in Coventry and Warwickshire Hospital, and was also involved in organising lectures and classes for the instruction of first aid, in connection with the St John Ambulance Association. Sophia originated this movement in Coventry in March 1882, and was Honorary Secretary until her death.

One of John's pastimes was to sketch landscapes and interesting buildings. He and his friend Nathaniel Troughton both left a legacy of views of old Coventry and the surrounding countryside. In May 1903, it was reported that John had met with an accident while gardening at his Priory Row address, slipping and injuring his left hip. He was just recovering from an earlier fall two weeks previously. It might seem strange now to report such an incident, but John Gulson was held in such high esteem within his Coventry, it was even reported that he had managed to get some sleep and was making a slow recovery! When John Gulson died on 25th December 1904, the obituaries in the local press ran to over 13 columns.

John Gulson's grave, quite Unassuming for one of Coventry's biggest benefactors.

The two main beneficiaries of John Gulson's will were Edward Burgess and John Gulson Burgess. These two brothers were John's nephews, the sons of Elizabeth his eldest sister. Edward Burgess inherited 'The Spring,' the property in Stoke, including the gardens, farm buildings, cottages and land. Edward, born in 1847, was an architect who specialised in the Gothic style that was in vogue at the time. Two well-known Coventry buildings, the Gulson Library and King Henry VIII Grammar School on Warwick Road were of his design. Even though only one of these buildings survives today, looking at old pictures of both, it becomes apparent that Edward was fond of a small turreted tower with a flag pole atop! Edward's elder brother John Gulson Burgess, inherited Stapleton Manor Farm in Leicestershire. Born in 1840, John was a barrister.

Other bequests in John's will included his library of books and illustrated works and a collection of etchings to the Corporation of the City. A bequest of £1,000 was made to Coventry and Warwickshire Hospital, to be used for the benefit of the Children's Ward. **Grave 9 Sq 28.**

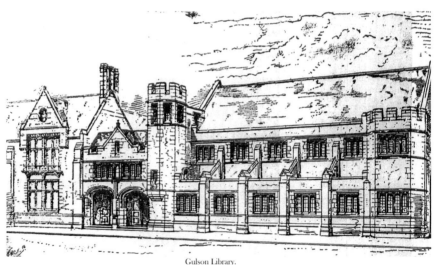

Gulson Library.

OSCAR HARMER

Oscar Harmer was born in America on 23rd October, 1849. He came to England after working for many years with American firms at a time when the machine tool practice used in American manufacturing was becoming more common. The American system of manufacturing was developed in the 19th century. Two main features of this method were the extensive use of interchangeable parts and the use of mechanisation to produce those parts. The system involved semi-skilled labour using machine tools and jigs to make standardised, interchangeable, identical parts. As the parts were interchangeable, companies were able to separate manufacture from assembly. Oscar Harmer introduced this system to the Coventry firm of Alfred Herbert's, making it possibly one of the first companies in England to adopt this system.

In 1897, while attending a lunch that was part of a bicycle show at Crystal Palace, Oscar met a business man who was in charge of a rapidly growing engineering firm in Coventry. His name was Alfred Herbert. At the time Oscar was managing the Capewell Horse Nail Company in Millwall. Shortly after this meeting Oscar went to work for Herbert and thus began a career in Coventry that was to lead to him becoming General Manager of Alfred Herbert's, a position he would keep until his death. One of his first tasks in this position was to initiate the building of a new foundry at Edgewick. This was to become the nucleus of all operations for the company in later years.

Many stories are told about Oscar by ex-employees and people who knew him. It is said he had 'a dignified presence accentuated by his beard!' His search for quality would sometimes lead him to smash work with a sledge hammer if it didn't reach his high standards.

Alfred Herbert wrote about his friend after his death in the Alfred Herbert News, the company's magazine. He said "I remember seeing him with his coat off, in the smithy, forging a lathe tool to exactly the shape he wanted while the smith looked on dumb-founded, and he was a man of picturesque language, but his criticisms, however drastic, were both given and taken in good part." Within the company as a whole, his influence was felt whether it be in the drawing office, works or commercial offices.

Oscar involved himself in all social aspects of the company, taking an interest in and attending many events, including football and rugby matches, swimming galas, golf competitions and even the model engineering club.

Oscar's funeral was held at Coventry Cathedral at 11:45 am on Monday 16th

October 1939. The funeral service was conducted by the Very Reverend R. T. Howard. A large congregation was in attendance including, of course, Sir Alfred Herbert and Lady Herbert and directors and many employees of the works. Over 150 wreaths were sent by his many friends within the company, around the country and other parts of the world.

When Oscar died he was 12 days short of his 91st birthday. Also interred here are Oscar's wife Hilda, who died 31st December 1934, aged 75, and Felix Stewart, husband of Gladys Harmer, who died 10th September 1953, aged 55.

Oscar Harmer is classed as one of Coventry's first great production managers.

Grave 5 Sq 77.

Oscar Harmer's funeral cortege entering the Cathedral.

Over 150 wreaths were sent from friends and family.

CHARLES JOHN HILL

Charles Hill JP belonged to one of the oldest watchmaking families of the Chapelfields area of the city. The family held a prominent position in business and public life. Charles's father William Henry Hill served on the town council for 51 years and was Mayor in the years 1871 and 1872.

Charles himself would go on to serve 36 years as a councillor, representing Earl Street Ward. He went on to serve as Mayor from 1889 to 1891 taking over the position from Albert Tomson, and handing over to George Singer. These were marked periods of industrial prosperity when the cycle trade was beginning to get into its stride in 1890. A consequence of this was many new factories and houses shot up in all areas. In particular the area of Hillfields was to develop at such a rate that in 12 months all available land in this area was built on.

For some time Charles was a director of the Coventry Cotton Company. He was also closely connected with the Corporation's electrical department, and was the first chairman of the committee for the Electric Light Department. Charles was made a city magistrate in 1897 and a County Justice in 1893.

Charles John Hill JP died on 15th November 1902, aged 65, at his residence "Elmfield" on Radford Road, a property he had built some years earlier. Charles had been suffering for some time from what was described as an internal complaint. He had undergone an operation for this complaint in London, which initially seemed to have gone well. However there was a rapid change in his condition and three days later he died of blood poisoning. His funeral service took place at Queens Road Chapel, where he and his family had worshipped. The service was taken by Rev W.E. Blomfield.

Charles's wife Emma died 12 years later on 3rd March 1914, aged 77. Her obituary in the Coventry and Warwickshire Graphic mentioned the many philanthropic causes that she was involved with. These included the Coventry and District Nursing Association, of which she was honorary secretary for a quarter of a century. She was also connected with the Coventry and Warwickshire Hospital and with the Lifeboat Association. Emma was buried with her husband in a grave which is topped with a large ornate sandstone monument. **Grave 8 Sq 43.**

ALICK HILL

On observing the grave of Charles and Emma Hill you cannot fail to notice the grave directly to the front of it as it looks very similar in design. On closer inspection you notice the name Alick Sargeant Hill JP. This is the grave of Charles and Emma's son Alick Hill. Alick was first and foremost a watchmaker, like others in his family. However in the early 1800s Alick moved away from this trade joining the Coventry Machinists Company Ltd. Later in life he wrote about his early working experiences in the 'Link,' the magazine of the Coventry Chain Co Ltd. He wrote " Somewhere between 1884 and 1888 a youth with a fair head of hair might frequently have been seen proceeding to his early morning work about 5:50am riding an old ordinary bicycle (chain-less) over cobbles at the bottom of Bishop Street, the slimy condition of which was responsible for more than one awful cropper. The coffee made in one's own tin over a gas jet at the back of the lathe on a cold winter's morning, breakfast cooked over the same jet, comprising a rasher with sometimes an egg, were amongst the nicest the writer can remember". After a few years, Alick was appointed manager of the firm's branch in Boston, U.S.A.

On returning from America, Alick felt confident enough to start a manufacturing business on his own. In 1896, he set up the Coventry Chain Company. Before this time, cycle chains were one of the few parts not made in Coventry. At first, the company was set up in Dale Street using steam power. The company expanded quickly as the demand for their products grew and eventually a move to a purpose-built factory in Spon End was necessary. The move was achieved with the company going public to raise the funds to do this.

Like his father, Alick became a city councillor. This was in 1914 and he represented Greyfriars Ward. When he became Mayor in 1916, Alick was taking on the office at one of most difficult times both for Coventry and England as a whole. Alick was seen to possess the right qualities to cope with the stresses and strains imposed by war, and the Council were unanimous in asking him to continue as mayor for an additional year. In fact, the Hill family were unique in Coventry's municipal history, with members of three generations becoming mayor: William, Charles and Alick. Alick was also made Justice of the Peace in 1918 and two years later he was made an Alderman.

One of the proudest moments of his duties as mayor must have been on 18th September 1917, when Queen Mary and Princess Mary visited Coventry to see the work of women and girls in the munition factories. The royal party also saw hostels and other centres set up for the workers' social welfare. Although, due to the war, the visit was a private one, the royal party was respectfully received by Alick and his wife Beatrice, in their roles as Mayor and Mayoress of Coventry.

In July 1920, Alick presented the city with a drinking fountain and horse trough with a memorial column dedicated to the 45 employees who lost their lives fighting during the First World War. The memorial was originally situated on Hearsall Common, but by 1999 it was rededicated in its new location at the front of the old works offices in Spon End. However, by this time all that remained was the memorial column.

Alick Sargeant Hill JP died on Wednesday 31st August 1921, at the relatively young age of 54. He died at Elmfield, the residence on Radford Road that his father had originally built. The funeral was attended by large crowds who lined the route to the Cemetery via Stoneleigh Terrace, St Patrick's Road, Parkside and London Road. Five hundred employees from the Coventry Chain Company followed the procession of coaches from the chapel to the Cemetery. At the Cemetery gates the cortège was met by the chief constable Mr W. Imber and 26 police officers who then headed the procession to the graveside. There were a great number of floral tributes including ones from members of the family, one from the City Council, and a large four-foot wreath from Coventry Chain employees, which was placed on the coffin.

Alick's wife Beatrice Louise was a native of Boston, USA. During her time as mayoress, Beatrice had taken a great interest in the post-war welfare of discharged soldiers and sailors. She was also interested in the local Prisoners of War Fund possibly due to the fact that the Hill's eldest son Arnold was held in the internment camp, Ruhleben, during most of the First World War. Beatrice also presented the city with a drinking fountain, which can still be seen today opposite the entrance to the War Memorial Park at the top of Warwick Road. When she died on 30th November 1936, aged 67, she had been ill for a few years. She actually died in a nursing home in Glasgow, which according to her obituary she had entered for an operation. Alick and Beatrice had three children, Arnold, Duncan, and Eileen. **Grave 41 Sq 35.**

ARNOLD HILL

It transpires that the reason their eldest son Arnold found himself in a German internment camp was due to the fact that he was in Berlin at the outbreak of war in 1914. Arnold was in Berlin working for the Coventry Chain Company, gaining experience in the manufacturing methods of Europe. He had previously spent some time in the tool-room back in Coventry and his father probably thought at the time sending him to Berlin was a good way for his son to acquire knowledge of new working methods to help within the company. The internment camp, Ruhleben, was situated on the site of a racecourse near Spandau and because it had been hastily constructed, the conditions were basic to say the least.

Although life in the camp was grim and harsh, it was later developed by its inmates into what was described as a 'mini-society' with a mix of athletic, cultural, artistic and educational associations. As Arnold was only 18 when he found himself interned, it is true to say that he was saved from life in the trenches, and all that came with it.

At the end of the war and after four years at Ruhleben, Arnold returned safely to Coventry and in the first issue of 'The Link' in 1919, this small piece was written. 'All will be glad to welcome amongst us again Mr. Arnold W. Hill, elder son of our managing director, who has recently returned to the Company from internment in Germany. The outbreak of war found him in Berlin enlarging his experiences, after having spent a short time in the tool-room. Hearty congratulations on his safe return have already been extended to him, and now, at the age of 22, he naturally finds it necessary to make up the leeway of the last four years.' In modern terms we might say he was fast-tracked through the various departments of the Company to get to management level.

Arnold was a very keen Rugby player, playing for Coventry Football Club, also playing at county level for the Warwickshire team. His proudest memory of his playing days was that he took part in the first game to be played at the Coundon Road ground.

He married Florence Austin in 1944; they had one son, Peter. Eventually Arnold became a director of the company associated in particular with the commercial side of the company. He resigned from the company when it became Renold Chain in 1930. Arnold then went on to join the Coventry firm John Morton and Son Ltd as a director. When Arnold died in December 1953, aged 57, his ashes were scattered on the grave of his parents. This also seems to be the case with his brother Duncan and sister Beatrice, who was usually known as Eileen. Within the kerb set on their parents' grave two tablets have been added showing that as well as Arnold who died in 1953, his brother Duncan died in May 1977, aged 77, and their sister Eileen died in January 1987, aged 80.

CHARLES WEBB ILLIFFE

Charles Webb Illiffe was born in Allesley Village, at the time a small village outside Coventry. Charles was christened on 4th December 1844, at St Michael's Church Coventry. His father, also called Charles, was a master draper with Coventry ribbon manufacturer Joseph Hands. His father was married to Mary Ann, nee Soden, in St Michael's Church in 1829. Mary's family had close connections with many city dignitaries of the day including two former Mayors, Thomas and Henry Soden.

Charles went to Coventry Grammar School, then to Oxford and finally went on to study medicine at Middlesex Hospital. After qualifying, Charles embarked on a three year tour of Canada to North and West British Columbia and whilst in the Rockies he learnt native languages from American Indians. He also visited California and South America. Perhaps this was the forerunner to the student gap year! On returning to Coventry in 1866, he set up a practice while living in Warwick Row, and in 1869 married Mary Ann in Birmingham. Charles worked his way up in the profession and was appointed Deputy Coroner for Warwickshire in 1882.

Having spent his childhood surrounded by the open countryside of Allesley, Charles looked for a place to build a large country manor as his home. The land that seemed ideal for this was near the River Sowe at Willenhall, on the main turnpike road from London. He called this house "The Chace." It was built in 1897, in a half timbered style as the country home of Dr Iliffe, and was used on many occasions to accommodate his large circle of friends and their staff. Charles also acquired land in St Michael's Parish, Stoke Green and the Gosford Green areas of Coventry. It was while living at The Chace that Charles could indulge in his passion for horses and people locally remembered him driving his governess cart that was drawn by a white pony. Charles also became known for his expert eye in judging horses, and would officiate at many important competitions, which included the annual Warwickshire Agricultural Society's show.

In 1899, Charles retired from medical practice to concentrate on municipal services and was so well established within the Council that the Liberals didn't oppose him in the 1910 elections for St Mary's Ward. Charles also held the position of Medical Officer to the Coventry Rural and District Council, and worked tirelessly for the poor of the city as Medical Officer for the Coventry Workhouse. For forty years Dr Iliffe served as Coventry Coroner, and later as justice of the peace. He also managed to find time to become Chairman of S & B

Gorton, cycle manufacturer! Charles's son William was to follow in his father's footsteps and became Coroner for Coventry in 1942.

Charles Webb Iliffe JP died on 1ˢᵗ March 1921, at the age of 77. Charles's wife Annie died 24ᵗʰ December 1939, at the age of 90. The inscription for Charles reads:-

'CHARLES WEBB ILIFFE
M.R.C.P
L.R.C.P
40 YEARS CORONER
FOR NORTH WARWICKSHIRE
DIED MARCH 1ST 1921
AGED 77'

Even though Charles's parents Charles and Ann are remembered on the headstone of this grave, the Cemetery records show that they are buried in a grave a few yards away from this one. Charles died on 26ᵗʰ April 1881, aged 77 and Ann died on 11ᵗʰ December 1893. Also inscribed under the inscription for Charles and Ann is the following:-

'THEIR SON
ROBERT AND HIS WIFE ELIZABETH
WHO WERE LOST AT SEA
1863'

The Chace in now a well established hotel and local landmark. It became a hotel in 1930. Whilst no longer in a rural setting you can still see an impressive building that would have once dominated the local landscape. **Grave 58 Sq 52.**

The Chace in more recent times   © IW.

ABE JEPHCOTT

Abraham William Jephcott had three passions in life: Coventry and its history, William Shakespeare, and the actress Dame Ellen Terry. It's not certain in which order these should be arranged, but I would like to think Coventry was first. It would be hard to find anyone so passionate about his city and its history, a history familiar to him in every street, building and corner. This knowledge was enhanced by a variety of Coventry-related antiques and items of interest collected by this proud citizen.

Reproduced with permission from Abe's family.

Abe was born in Smithford Street in December 1885 to Abraham and Frances Jephcott. The family home stood where the circular café now stands in the Lower Precinct.

Although born in Smithford Street, Abe spent much of his life at 102 Stoney Stanton Road, the place where his father ran his business from. Abe attended St Peter's School, Hillfields from 1897 to 1903 and later became a member of the 'Old Scholars' association. By the age of ten, Abe was attending Wheatley Street School, and decided to leave, which he did. In a newspaper interview in 1959, he is quoted as saying: 'They dragged me back, of course, but I soon found a way out. In those days you could obtain a 'labour ticket'- a kind of scholastic certificate-which allowed you to leave. I got it and left for good at the age of 13.' Abe then started his first job, pouring lemonade into bottles to be sold at Coventry's Great Fair. Asked why he had taken such a job his reply was that he was fascinated by the lovely coloured mineral water sparkling in the bottles. It was after the fair left town that Abe was apprenticed to his father, in the family trade as a builder, making bakery ovens. On completion of his apprenticeship, Abe became a freeman of the city. Eventually, Abe took the business over from his father and continued to work there for many years.

An interesting story about Abe in the days of his youth involves Abe and two of his friends who were interested in keeping fit and would often use walking as a mode of training. In 1907, a famous weight-lifting champion was due to appear in London and all three friends decided to walk to London to see him! This was a task that took them 24 hours, and some of this was undertaken barefoot, due to the discomfort of their boots. Abe later spent some time in the Army, with the Royal Engineers. He admitted to being a 'mediocre' soldier saying he was glad to get back from Greece and Macedonia after the First World War.

Abe wrote many articles for 'The Guildsman', a monthly journal published for the Freemen of Coventry. Books relating to some of the more unusual aspects of Coventry's history were one of Abe's specialities. For many years Abe worked on 'The Godiva Scroll' which was made from leather and recorded the names of well known Coventrians and people of national importance. The scroll was decorated by Abe with illustrations and relics he collected over the years. It took him around four years to make the scroll and in it he included an original Anglo Saxon poem featuring the story of Lady Godiva. Over the years it was signed by many Coventry mayors and also people said to be descended from Lady Godiva herself. Strangely, there is one notable name missing from the scroll - that of Abe himself. Abe also kept a record of old Coventrians who had written to him from the far corners of the world.

Abe's interest in Dame Ellen Terry probably came from the fact that she was a famous Coventrian, but this happened quite by chance. Her parents were travelling actors and were staying in Market Street, Coventry at the time of her birth, 27th February 1847. Ellen Terry was one of the finest Shakespearean actresses from the late 1870s. Abe was for many years a leading member of the Ellen Terry Fellowship, a small group of people who kept alive the memory of the famous actress. Abe had a great passion for Shakespeare, travelling many a time to Stratford-upon-Avon to attend productions of Shakespeare's works at the Royal Shakespeare Theatre. Abe would be accompanied by his wife Clara, nee Stringer, whom he married at St Peter's Church, Hillfields in 1915, and also with them would be their two daughters, Sonia and Audrey. Clara worked for many years at Cash's, the famous Coventry ribbon maker, eventually becoming a manageress. Abe's passion for the theatre certainly influenced his daughters who, in later life continued to enjoy a night at the theatre in Stratford-upon-Avon. Two of Abe's great-nephews are in fact well known actors: Saul and Dominic Jephcott both trained at RADA and have both had successful careers on stage and screen. Saul has more film credits to his name, while Dominic's TV work has included the long running dramas Casualty and Holby City. Both were born in Coventry and attended Binley Park School.

Another of Abe's interests was reading and writing poetry. Here is a short piece that appeared in a small book he wrote called 'Know Your Coventry':

Coventry! Coventry, my heart is yours,
I left no kiss on foreign shores'
Old world Cities of Eastern hue,
Dipp'n in the charms of midnight blue,
And sungold Isles in the Aegean Sea,
Were barren and cold to a lover like me.

Because my love was Coventry born,
Never to fade nor be foresworn,
While the blush of a Yuletide fire,
Tempts the snowflakes to kiss and conspire,
On the window panes of my old street,
Where topless towers on castles meet,

And melt within the native eye,
When the Shepherd's star draws high.

Abe was able to combine his passion for Coventry's history and its old buildings in the 1950s when he was given the job of restoring Ford's Hospital in Greyfriars Lane. This building had been severely damage during the bombing raids of the Second World War, and through Abe's passion and attention to detail this building was saved for future generations to admire. Also, when the city centre was being re-developed after the Second World War, he fought hard to make sure the name Smithford Street would be preserved in some way, and was said to be very pleased with the eventual use of Smithford Way as a new Coventry thoroughfare.

Abe died aged 85, on 13th February, 1971. He had been living with his daughter Audrey and her husband in Avon Street, Coventry. It is ironic to think that he would pass away in a street named after the river in Stratford, the birthplace of his beloved Shakespeare. Abe's funeral service was held at St Peter's Church on Wednesday the 17th February at 2:15pm followed by the interment at the Cemetery. Even though the names of Abe and Clara are the only names inscribed on the headstone, they were not the first burials. Abe's parents are also buried here: Frances, who died in October 1936, aged 74 and Abraham who died in March 1945, aged 82. Clara died in 1973, aged 85. The headstone is a small simple stone as, according to his daughter, Audrey, 'Abe didn't like the look of the tall dark headstones usually found in cemeteries'. Inscribed are these words which were originally coloured in Coventry blue:-

**'ABE JEPHCOTT
HISTORIAN
1885-1971
AND HIS BELOVED WIFE
CLARA JEPHCOTT
1888-1973'**

The ashes of Audrey's husband, Abe's other daughter Sonia, and her husband are also interred in this grave. **Grave 32 Sq 78.**

FRED LEE

In 1881, Fred Lee was apprenticed to his father who was also called Fred, as a watch-jewel manufacturer, at the family firm Fred Lee and Co of Dover Street. On completion of his apprenticeship in 1888, Fred became a Freeman of Coventry. Fred's knowledge of the watch industry was great and he travelled extensively in this connection to America, Canada, Switzerland and Italy. Fred didn't actually retire from the watch trade until he was 80.

By 1892, Fred had become secretary of the Licensed Victuallers Association, a position he kept until 1947. Fred was also a Freemason: a member of Coventry Foundation and St. Barbara's Lodges. In 1904, he became chairman of the directors of Coventry City Football Club, and was later elected president in 1920.

During the First World War, Fred made an important contribution to the war effort. In 1915, the Admiralty Compass Department consulted Fred when a crisis arose concerning pivots and jewel caps used in aero-compasses. The problem caused the compasses to read inaccurately. Fred, with his many years experience in these matters, solved the problem by developing a patent which was later adopted by British, French and American manufacturers. Because of the sensitive nature of this patent, the manufacturing of all pivots and caps at Dover Street works was placed under the Official Secrets Act.

Fred Lee first became a member of the City Council in 1907 and made his mark by becoming chairman of many committees within the council, and being appointed an alderman in 1921. This proud Coventrian was first elected mayor of Coventry on 9th November, 1926 and his 19 years of experience held him in good stead for the role before him. This moment must have been tinged with sadness as Fred's wife Eliza had died in the July of that year. Eliza Lee had passed away peacefully on the morning of Saturday, 31st July, at their home Hawarden Lodge, Holyhead Road. According to the local press she had been ill for the previous two years, yet it was not disclosed what her illness was. It was said that she had at all times supported Fred in all his political and business endeavours. Eliza's funeral service took place at Coventry Cathedral, followed by the interment at the Cemetery. As a result of this, when Fred became mayor, his daughter Gladys Denbigh Lowis took on the duties of Mayoress. On the day he was elected as mayor, Fred also attended a presentation in his honour at his business premises in Dover Street. His employees presented him with a watch engraved with the words: 'Presented to Alderman Fred Lee JP by the employees and staff of Messrs Fred Lee and Co. on being elected Mayor of the City of Coventry. November 9th 1926'.

One of Fred's proudest moments as Mayor must have been on Saturday 8th October 1927, when he headed the civic party that welcomed Earl Haig to the War Memorial Park for the unveiling and dedication of the War Memorial. The park was first opened on 9th July 1921, and the Memorial was in remembrance of the 2,587 men of the city who had laid down their lives in the First World War. The ceremony was attended by an estimated crowd of 50,000.

In his second term as Mayor in 1928, Fred had many duties to perform. In February, he unveiled a tablet in Spencer Park dedicated to David Spencer, the generous benefactor who had gifted the park to the people of Coventry. He also planted a tree called a Verdun Oak, so named because it had grown in Coventry Corporation nurseries from an acorn picked up from the battlefield of Verdun in 1916. The tree was significant because it replaced a temporary cenotaph that had been erected by ex-servicemen of Coventry after the First World War. The temporary structure had been removed when the permanent War Memorial was erected in the Memorial Park. On Tuesday 17th July 1928, Fred took part in the unveiling of new boundary markers on the extension of the City boundary. It was a busy day starting from the Council House at 9:30 am, with the first unveiling at 9:40: the Gibbet Hill Boundary Stone. There were seven stones altogether, the last being the Willenhall Bridge Boundary Stone unveiled at 12:35.

In January 1930, Fred unexpectedly became mayor for a third time. Alderman Alfred Makepeace, the mayor at the time, had died suddenly in the previous December. A special meeting had to be held to decide who would complete the mayoral year. Before a decision could be made, the mayoral mace was draped in black, according to tradition. Fred was voted in, receiving 39 votes, with only 13 votes going to his opponent, JA Moseley. As Fred had recently occupied the position of mayor, it was thought that he would be the right person to take up the reins. He obviously knew the role well and his daughter Gladys was willing to take on the duties of mayoress once more. It was to be a very eventful year. In March 1930 Fred, as Mayor, took great pleasure in accepting the gift of a collection of water-colour paintings by Herbert Edward Cox. The paintings had been bought a few months earlier by David Cooke, a prosperous tobacconist in the town and director of Coventry City Football Club. These beautiful paintings depicted a fast disappearing Coventry and the pictures are still on display in the Council House to this day, although many of the streets and buildings shown in them have now gone.

In May 1930, the city celebrated 'Coventry Flying Week', and Fred became the first mayor to take an aerial flight over the city. He and a civic party boarded the big Handley Page airliner named 'Prince Harry' and in a flight lasting just ten minutes, they covered a ten-mile circuit of the city. On the 13th August of that same year, Fred embarked on another prestigious journey. Accompanied by his son Horace, he travelled on the Cunard liner Ascania from Southampton to Canada. The itinerary included visits to Quebec, Ottawa, Montreal, Toronto and Niagara Falls. The purpose of the trip was to strengthen industrial links and observe new manufacturing processes.

Incidentally, Fred's son Horace had played Rugby football at its highest level for Coventry and Warwickshire and, at the time, was considered to be the best left wing to play at town and county level. Unfortunately, his career was cut short by a severe knee injury. November saw Fred unveiling new stained glass windows donated by Mr. W. Coker Iliffe, in St. Mary's Hall. At the end of his year as Mayor, Fred was given great thanks in speeches from the Council, for stepping in after the death of Alderman Makepeace. In reply to this, Fred said it had again been an honour to serve the city that he loved so much and listed some of the memorable events he had been involved with whilst Mayor.

Fred Lee died on 16th January, 1950. He was aged 82, and his death was described as 'sudden'. At the time of his death he was the oldest member on the council and as such was referred to as the 'Father' of the council. His funeral service took place in Holy Trinity Church, and was attended by people from every aspect of the city's life, headed by the Mayor and Mayoress Alderman and Mrs V. A. Hammond. The church was full to capacity and not only was there a large representation from the City Council, but people representing many other organisations were present: from the city, the county and also Birmingham. The prayers were led by the Vicar of Holy Trinity, Canon G. W. Clitheroe. Acting as bearers were six officers of the Coventry City Police Force. There was a brief and simple ceremony at the Cemetery, with around 100 people present at the graveside who all joined in the singing of the first and last verses of 'Abide With Me.' Masses of flowers were laid out on the stretch of green nearby.

The first part of the inscription on his impressive memorial concerns Fred's wife Eliza who died on 31st July 1926, aged 57. A square piece has been added to the base and this is for Spencer Lee JP (Fred) who was Fred and Eliza's other son, who died on 11th December, 1996, and this where his ashes were interned. Around the right hand side of the memorial is an inscription for Robert (Bob) Bellas Lowis who died 28th August 1937, aged 48. This is Fred's son-in-law and husband to his daughter Gladys who had accompanied her father as Mayoress.

Robert Bellas Lowis is actually buried in the plot directly next to Fred and Eliza, making it a double width. Bob Lowis, as he was known to most people, was 48 when he died. Before the outbreak of the First World War, Bob had worked at the Standard Motor Co. He enlisted in 'C' Battery, 2nd Brigade, Royal Field Artillery, and then on to the Midland Howitzer Brigade, Royal Field Artillery. He was offered a commission but preferred to stay with his comrades as their sergeant. He saw service at Ypres and the Somme, being in the advance to the Hindenburg Line. He fought at the third battle of Ypres where he was severely wounded and because of this he was eventually discharged from the forces and unfortunately was unable to resume his work at the Standard Motor Co. Following his funeral service at Coventry Cathedral, on 1st September, 1937, the cortège moved on to the Cemetery where it was met at the gates by some old comrades who formed a guard of honour. One of those present was Corporal Hutt V.C. representing the 7th Warwicks Old Comrades.

The name of Fred Lee is still remembered in Coventry due to the naming of a road in the Stivichall area of the city as Fred Lee Grove. **Grave 1 Sq 20.**

CHARLES AND GEORGE LIPSCOMB

No one could foresee how Wednesday 7th January would end, when two young brothers Charles and George Lipscomb boarded the 12:25pm train from Coventry Station bound for Kenilworth. Once they had alighted from the train at Kenilworth Station they walked to Stoneleigh Park with the intention of skating on the frozen River Avon. During the Christmas and New Year holiday of 1890-91 a hoar-frost and ice had descended. Even though the river was frozen the dangers of this fast flowing river were well known to locals.

The family had only recently moved to Coventry from Leamington, and were residing at 35, Hertford Street. The boys' father was the Rev Edwin Francis Lipscomb who had come to the City for the position of Clerk in Holy Orders.

When the boys walked into Home Park they left their overcoats near the new bridge, and attached their skates, moving onto the frozen river where they would have spent about an hour enjoying themselves. Frank Burbury of Crewe Farm saw them both laughing and talking.

Some minutes after, Mr Burbury heard a shriek and on running to the river bank he discovered that the elder brother was missing while the younger was engaged in a frantic struggle in the icy water. Both boys had gone through the ice at the centre of the Avon, and even though Mr Burbury was able to talk to the younger brother there was no way of rescuing the boy. He soon followed his brother through the ice to his death.

Both bodies were retrieved by workers from the estate, and taken to the riding school at Stoneleigh Abbey. This tragic event was a terrible shock for Lord and Lady Leigh and the rest of the household.

It was late in the evening before the parents were contacted and the only way to identify the boys was from the name Lipscomb on the collar of one of their shirts. Mr and Mrs Lipscomb travelled to Stoneleigh the same evening to identify the bodies of Charles and George.

Charles Lipscomb was 22 years of age, and a student of St. Augustine's Missionary College, Canterbury, and had recently been accepted for missionary work in North-West Canada, with the intention for him to leave England the next July. George Lipscomb was 16 years of age and in term time would have been at boarding school. Both boys were said to be fine looking young men for their age, the elder being 5ft 10in, with the younger being 5ft 7in.

Inquests were held the following day, in a room that adjoined the riding school. The enquiries were led by Dr Wynter. The Rev. and The Hon Canon Leigh was foreman of the jury. The verdict was declared as a fatal accident for both.

The brothers' bodies were transferred from Stoneleigh Abbey on the Thursday evening to lie at the parents' house at Hertford Street in the City. The funeral took place at 3:00pm on Saturday 10th January at the Cemetery and the vicar of Holy Trinity the Rev. the Hon. W. R. Verney officiated. Floral tributes were sent from their parents, two from the boys' sisters, two from Lord Leigh, and some from fellow students of George Lipscomb. Numerous letters of condolence were forwarded to the bereaved family, among them letters from Lord Leigh, the Dean of York, and the Dean of Chester. The coffins were covered with wreaths, and at the foot of each were hung the skates that the brothers had been wearing at the time of the accident. The inscription on the memorial stone reads:-

'ERECTED
BY FELLOWS AND STUDENTS OF
St AUGUSTINES COLLEGE
CANTERBURY
TO THE MEMORY OF
CHARLES LANGFORD LIPSCOMB
AGED 22 YEARS
STUDENT OF St AUGUSTINES COLLEGE
AND HIS BROTHER
GEORGE LANGFORD BROOK LIPSCOMB
AGED 16 YEARS
WHO WERE DROWNED WHILE SKATING
ON THE AVON IN STONELEIGH PARK
JANUARY 7TH 1891
R.I.P.'

This stone was erected in May 1891 by student friends of Charles. This impressive memorial of Italian marble, a cross on three bases, and the inscription was originally in gold. The stone was prepared and erected by G.L.Taylor of Far Gosford Street. **Grave 40 Sq 85.**

JOHN BAIRD LOUDON

John Baird Loudon was born in Ayr Scotland in February 1823. When he became Mayor of Coventry in 1894, he was to be the first Scotsman to hold this office in the city.

John first came to Coventry in 1861 to open a shoe shop in Cross Cheaping on behalf of Messrs R and J Dick, boot and shoe manufacturers of Glasgow.

He served as Mayor from November 1894 to November 1896. This was the start of the cycle boom in the town. He was a great advocate of the use of electric light and it was because of his interest that it was introduced in Coventry in 1896.

John was made a city magistrate in 1893 and County Justice in 1897. An interesting and somewhat amusing story relating to John's time as Mayor concerns the first motor car to be driven in Coventry. In May 1896, a French engineer named Léon Bollée drove his 'autocar' up and down Hertford Street. The machine was described as a 'Tricar': a tandem tricycle with two wheels at the front that steered the machine. Alderman Loudon was invited to ride as a passenger and was taken along Kenilworth Road. It was reported that the machine reached speeds of 20 miles per hour!

John Loudon J P died 13ᵗʰ October 1910, aged 87. His wife Elizabeth died just two months later in December 1910, aged 86. At the time of their deaths, their address was Roslyn Villa, Warwick Road. Also interred in this grave are John and Elizabeth's sons: George who died in 1868, aged 13 months and Henry, who died in 1898, aged 42. **Grave 33 Sq 95.**

Buried in a grave nearby is Arthur another son, who died in 1914, aged 48.

ALFRED MAKEPEACE

Alfred Makepeace, like his father was a Coventrian and was born in Gosford Street in 1863. As a youngster, Alfred attended the Convent School at Gosford Green. His later education was at Weston Hall School, near Rugby.

At 21, Alfred passed the exam of the Pharmaceutical Society and qualified as a chemist. However, this was not destined to be his eventual career. Alfred entered Guys Hospital London, to study dental surgery and after three years gained his diploma in dentistry. While studying at Guy's he enjoyed the privilege of playing in the famous hospital's Rugby fifteen and also keeping wicket for the cricket eleven.

In 1893, Alfred returned to Coventry to open his own dental practice. Only a year later he was appointed honorary dental surgeon at the Coventry and Warwickshire Hospital. Alfred was to hold this post for 34 years.

His sporting interests continued when back in Coventry, with fishing and golf being his main pastimes. Alfred was captain of both Finham and Hearsall Golf Clubs. Salmon fishing was his real passion however and this is something that he was to indulge in when on holiday. He landed prime salmon whilst in Scotland, Ireland and Norway. Alfred was also a fairly regular visitor to Highfield Road, keenly watching the progress of Coventry City F.C.

Alfred Makepeace first entered civic life in the city in 1910, when he was elected as a representative of Greyfriars Ward, being re-elected in 1913. He was made a Justice of the Peace in 1918 and an Alderman in 1923. He was on many committees including the Watch Committee, Public Health Committee, and was Chairman of the Baths and Parks Committee.

In October 1928, Albert resigned his position as dental surgeon from the hospital to devote his time to his political ambitions and on November 9th of the same year, Albert had the great honour of becoming Mayor of Coventry. He was, in fact the first Roman Catholic Mayor of Coventry since the Reformation. However, late in the following year, Albert became ill with pneumonia and died on the 19th December at his home, Styvechale Lodge Kenilworth Road. Incidentally, he was the tenth mayor of Coventry to have died in office in 581 years. Previous to this was in June 1924, when Alderman William Hewitt had died, and the last Mayor to die in office before these two aldermen was William Eburne in 1791.

The funeral of Alfred Makepeace was held on 23rd December 1928. In accordance with the tradition of the Roman Catholic Church, his coffin rested overnight before the high altar of St Osburg's church, draped in the Mayoral robes. Alfred had been a prominent worshipper at St Osburg's and the church was crowded with people paying their respects to a man who had served fellow citizens so well. After a Requiem Mass, the first portion of the burial service was said. The lengthy cortège of around 50 cars slowly threaded its way through the city via Smithford Street, Broadgate, Earl Street and Much Park Street onto the London Road and entrance to the Cemetery. The cortège was escorted by members of the Police and Fire Brigade as it passed through the city centre where thousands of citizens had assembled to pay their last respects on route.

This was a very sad time for the Mayoress, as this was a double bereavement. Her brother, Harvey Clifford Perkins, known as 'Perky' had died on December 7th, aged 44, after a long illness. His name is inscribed on the same headstone as Alfred, but records show he is buried in the plot next to his brother in law and was buried 13 days before, on the 10th December.

An unusual meeting took place early in January 1930, when it was necessary to appoint a new Mayor following the sudden death of Alderman Makepeace. It was decided to elect Alderman Fred Lee for the remainder of the term. Alderman Lee was thought by all as a good choice having already held this office from 1926-28, and as he had not long relinquished the role it would be easier for him to take over the position again.

The memorial on the grave is quite impressive. Made from pink marble, the top takes on the form of a bird bath. With all the bird life in the Cemetery it is nice to see such a useful and practical monument. **Grave 98 Sq 19.**

A welcome refreshment stop for the birdlife.   Picture IW.

JAMES MURRAY

James Murray was born in Armagh Ireland on 9th December 1831, and kept himself very busy in his short life. He left Ireland to work in England and was articled as an architect to Walter Scott in Liverpool. For a short period from 1856 James was in partnership with Edward Welby Pugin the most eminent of Victorian architects. It appears that James was most productive as an architect in the Coventry area from the mid 1850s till 1863.

Some of his more notable works in Coventry included: the Corn Exchange 1856, Blue Coat School 1857, St. Michael's Baptist Chapel 1858, Stoneleigh Terrace and The School of Art which was opened by Sir Joseph Paxton in 1863.

The Corn Exchange was built in Hertford Street at a cost of £8000 and opened in June 1856. It was used primarily for the buying and selling of corn, but was also a venue for concerts and meetings. It was here in December 1856, that a certain Charles Dickens recited 'A Christmas Carol'. The building was impressive in its original form; it had stabling in the basement for horses and carriages. The building was later redesigned as the Empire Theatre, which was damaged in the wartime bombing of 1940. The basement is all that is left of this building, latterly called the Dog and Trumpet.

Blue Coat School still exists next to Holy Trinity, and recently underwent a great deal of restoration as part of the millennium project in the area. However, it is sad to reflect that this appears to be the only piece of architecture remaining in the town centre designed by James Murray.

St Michael's Baptist Chapel was destroyed in wartime bombing in 1940; however the roofless shell was used as a static water tank for the remainder of the war.

Stoneleigh Terrace was a beautiful row of terraced houses, designed in the Gothic style which ran along the top of Greyfriars Green on Queens Road. They were very prestigious when built, attracting the likes of George Singer and James himself living there. They were lost with the building of the Ring Road.

The School of Art on the corner of Ford Street and Hales Street was also demolished to make way for the new Ring Road in the late 1960s. This was a magnificent building with striking carvings above the windows, one of which was saved and is now on display in the Herbert Art Gallery.

Many other buildings are attributed to Murray in Coventry and the surrounding area from the late 1850s, including the three almshouses in Stoneleigh. James also had offices in Liverpool and in the Strand London.

James Murray died on 14th December 1863, aged 32, of consumption. He was still living at Stoneleigh Terrace at the time. His monument is of a Gothic Revival style. The spire is coloured in bands of sandstone and three panels sit at the base with reliefs of a sculptor, an architect, and artist in a similar style to those on the School of Art. His friend Pugin attended his funeral and when looking at the monument it is interesting to wonder if he played a part in its design. **Grave 1 Sq 77.**

NEWSOME MEMORIAL

The Newsome family is known to have been in Coventry for more than 400 years and members of that family have been at the forefront of many industries and have made many civic connections for most of that time.

Jabez Newsome was in partnership with ribbon manufacturer Charles Bray. Jabez died on 28th March 1889, aged 70. At the time he was living in Spon Street in a weaver's house which in recent years has been restored as a small working museum project. Hannah his wife died on 30th October 1878, and it is her father who had originally owned the weaving property in Spon Street.

ISAAC JABEZ THEO NEWSOME

Isaac Jabez Theo Newsome was by trade a watchmaker and for a time was in partnership with Samuel Yeomans, trading as Newsome and Yeomans. Isaac eventually traded on his own or with the help of his sons. He was a member of the Watchmakers Protection Association, at one point being its president.

In June 1885, Isaac stood as a Conservative candidate for the council and won Earl Street Ward remaining as a councillor for the rest of his life. He was a member of the Board of Guardians in Coventry, thus being responsible for the well-being of the inmates of the Workhouse, and became chairman in 1883. Isaac was a strong churchman and a generous supporter and helper of St Thomas's Earlsdon. Isaac died on 13th January 1891, aged 51, of a chest and lung condition at his home 21, Spon Street. His wife Elizabeth died on the 4th March 1898, aged 63.

SAMUEL THEO NEWSOME

Elizabeth and Isaac's son Samuel Theo Newsome was born in April 1868 and was educated privately. Samuel was said to possess a fine singing voice and his father had wanted him to take up a musical career. However, he became a watch manufacturer entering his father's business and after serving his apprenticeship became a Freeman of Coventry.

A keen sportsman, Samuel at one time played Rugby Football for Coventry, being a member of the team that won the Midland Counties Cup in the early

1890s. He was also a keen fisherman and cricketer.

In 1892, Samuel married Kate Purnell; she was the daughter of Edward Purnell, who was City Engineer for Coventry Council for forty years.

In 1904, as the watch trade began to decline, Samuel, along with some partners bought Coventry Hippodrome Theatre. At the time the theatre was no more than a large tin building on the Pool Meadow area in the town centre. One of Samuel's partners in this venture was Robert Halpin, later to be Alderman Halpin. Within a couple of years the tin building was replaced with a new theatre opposite the site of the old one, in Hales Street. Samuel Theo Newsome held the position of chairman and managing director of the theatre until he died.

Samuel Theo Newsome died on Saturday 4th January 1930 aged 61, at his home 'Fairhill', Warwick Road. The funeral service was held at St Thomas's Church, Earlsdon and was conducted by Reverend H. C. James. A large cross of white flowers from his widow Kate was placed on top of the coffin. The coffin itself was of polished Warwickshire oak enclosing an elm shell. The funeral was attended by many of Samuel's business and sporting associates along with a large representation of the family. The arrangements for the funeral were carried out by W. Smith and Son, of Friar Road Coventry.

Samuel's eldest son, Theo Edward Newsome was educated at King Henry VIII School in Coventry and later studied at Birmingham University. After leaving University he went to work for the Daimler Company. In early August 1914, he enlisted in the army and later that month Theo was sent to France. By December 1914, he had been promoted to the rank of corporal. After receiving his commission in July the same year, he joined the 2nd Battalion, Royal Warwickshire Regiment and became a Second Lieutenant. Sadly, Theo was killed in action on 25th September 1915 at Loos. He was 21. Part of this grave has a cross in memory of Theo, with his Regimental badge inscribed along with his name. As well as this memorial there is a tree with a plaque dedicated to Theo in the Coventry War Memorial Park. Theo has no known grave but is also commemorated on the Loos Memorial in France.

SAMUEL HERBERT NEWSOME

Samuel's other son Samuel Herbert Newsome known as Sam, was born in June 1901. Sam became joint managing director of the Coventry Hippodrome Company after his father's death.

Prior to taking over from his father Sam Newsome started his own business at the age of 22. He started building and tuning sports and racing cars and was subsequently appointed distributor of S.S. Cars, later to become Jaguar Cars and Sam's company soon had three depots. From 1925, Sam took part in many international car races in the works teams of Lea Francis, Riley and Aston Martin. He was successful with these teams six times in the Le Mans 24 hour race in the 1930s. The company also distributed motorcycles in the early days.

In 1935, Sam planned and built a new theatre to replace the Old Hippodrome. The new Coventry Hippodrome opened in November 1937 and at the time it was one of the largest and best equipped theatres in the country. Because of his success in running the Coventry Hippodrome, Sam became a successful impresario and during the 1940s he was offered directorships at companies such as Moss Empires and Associated Theatre Properties which controlled several West End theatres and venues all over the country.

Sam Newsome's other activities included being Justice of the Peace, for Warwickshire, being President of the Midland Automobile Club, 1955-1965 and in 1954 he even found time to be Captain of Coventry Golf Club for the year. In 1965, Sam was initiated into the Companionship of the Grand Order of Water Rats by Tommy Trinder. Sam sold his interests in the Coventry Hippodrome Theatre in 1967 for the sum of £200,000.

Sam Newsome died in 1970, aged 68 and was referred to in his obituary as 'Mr Coventry Theatre'. Sam had been ill for some time and a few days before he died had been transferred to Whitley Hospital from his home on Kenilworth Road.

Sam's wife, Pauline Grant Newsome died on 22nd October 1986, aged 71. Pauline came from a theatrical background, with a career that had covered half a century. She worked at the People's Theatre in St Pancras, North London, and was well known for her work with Glyndebourne, Sadler's Wells and the English National Opera. As a choreographer, Pauline specialised in opera ballet and the movement of opera singers whilst on stage. However, in Coventry she would always be best remembered for writing and producing the annual pantomime at the Coventry Theatre, which she did for over ten years during the 1950s and 60s. Pauline was Sam Newsome's third wife. **Grave 11 Sq 37.**

EDWARD HENRY PETRE
LADY GWENDOLINE PETRE

Edward Henry Petre J.P. of Whitley Abbey died on Friday 21ˢᵗ November 1902, aged 71. Edward Henry Petre J.P. was the third son of Henry William Petre, of Dunkenhalgh, Lancashire, and belonged to one of the oldest Roman Catholic families in the country. His residence, Whitley Abbey, was situated on the outskirts of Coventry and Edward purchased the estate from Viscount Hood in 1867. At the time, it amounted to over 250 acres. Part of the house had been rebuilt in 1834, but it was greatly improved by Edward, who also added a chapel. The Petre family were the last people to use the Abbey as a family home.

Though Edward was never a very public man, at different times he held a number of important offices in Coventry and Warwickshire and for many years he was Deputy Lieutenant of Warwickshire. He was made a county magistrate in 1867, city justice in 1873, and was a High Sheriff of Warwickshire in 1877.

In his early life, he was a captain in the Lancashire Yeomanry Hussars, and while at Whitley frequently showed an interest in the local Volunteer forces. Edward was reported to be a man of kindly and benevolent disposition, and was well liked by all who had contact with him. He would often place the grounds of Whitley Abbey at the disposal of the people of Coventry for parties or gatherings of deserving local groups. He was a generous supporter of St Osburg's and St Mary's Churches in Coventry.

Edward was specially remembered for his work with the inmates of the Workhouse. Hardly a week would pass without some kindness from Edward towards them and he would often send presents of clothes and food. Even in the last weeks of his life, when ill in London he still did not forget the inmates. In addition to this, Edward and his wife Lady Gwendoline took a great interest in the Infant Life Society, and the nursing of children in the Workhouse.

When Edward died he had been ill for several months with heart problems, and some weeks beforehand had gone to London for specialist treatment, and this is where he died.

The household at Whitley Abbey had received a telegram announcing his death. Edward Petre's funeral was noted for an absence of extravagance. His coffin had rested overnight in St Osburg's Church, after its journey by train from London the previous day. Then, in accordance with his wishes, one of the farm wagons from Whitley Abbey was used as conveyance from St Osburg's to the Cemetery, instead of an ordinary hearse. The wagon was heavily draped, with two shire horses attached, each being attended by a servant of the deceased. The bearers walked either side en route to the Cemetery. The route was lined with spectators, and several business establishments showed signs of mourning. At the entrance to the Cemetery there was a large number of citizens in attendance, the coffin was placed on a bier with the procession to the grave being a short distance. The bearers were all servants from Whitley Abbey.

Lady Gwendoline Petre of Whitley Abbey died in September 1910, aged 74. Lady Gwendoline was a member of the Talbot family, another of the important Roman Catholic families in England. This makes her family background most interesting. The Talbots are the Earls of Shrewsbury and can be traced back to Richard Talbot who fought with William the Conqueror at the Battle of Hastings. The Talbot's family seat was Alton Towers and Lady Gwendoline's younger brother inherited the property and lived there, but died young at the age of 23. The Talbot family are also connected with the cars of this name.

Lady Gwendoline was a member of the Coventry Boarding Out Committee which was responsible for the organisation of foster care of children in the workhouse. For many years she and her husband took a great deal of interest in the well-being of children of whom the authority had supervision. **Grave 1 Sq 19.**

Whitley Abbey was used to house refugees during World War I, some of whom are buried in the Cemetery. The Abbey passed down the Petre family, but was never occupied by the family and fell into disrepair. After World War II, the site was sold to Coventry City Council and later the building of Whitley Abbey Comprehensive School was started. The school is now known as Whitley Academy.

FRED POOLE

Fred Walter Poole was a well known grocer of Fleet Street, who had built up a good reputation as a supplier of all aspects of the grocery trade. Fred had come to Coventry as a young man of 19 years to start as an assistant to Arthur Atkins another well respected member of the grocery and provision trade.

As well as being heavily involved with the grocery trade, Fred was on the Board of Guardians for Schools, and was very active in church matters particularly with St John's and for several years served in the office of parish warden.

On School Board matters the question of religious education was of upmost importance. In 1894, he was elected as a guardian of the poor for St Michael's Within, and was noted for his excellent service. It was in this role for St Michael's that his knowledge of provisions made him a valued member of the Stores Committee. Part of his role was to control what was provided for the workhouse.

Although his Fleet Street premises served him well, Fred was not one to pass up a good business opportunity, so when he had the chance to buy another shop he became the owner of a premises in Earlsdon. It was situated on the corner of Moor Street and Warwick Street in what was then a small suburb. The shop in question had been originally opened by Samuel Ward, and was actually Earlsdon's first shop.

Fred lived and worked in Coventry for forty years and in that time he would have seen great changes in the demand for his wares, as the town expanded during the 19th century.

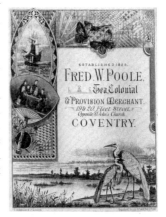

For around twelve months, Fred suffered poor health brought on by a heart condition. Frederick Walter Poole died on 7th July 1897, aged 59. Twenty five years later Fred's wife Ann Maria died on 2nd February 1922, aged 76. Sadly, the daughter of Fred and Ann was the first to be buried in this grave. Her name was Edith Caroline and she died in May 1873, aged six months.

Grave 42 Sq 180.

GEORGE RAINBOW

George Rainbow was the licensee of The Admiral Codrington, near Coventry Canal Basin and before that he was a representative for Phillips and Marriott's brewery. He was well known as a prominent member of the Liberal Party in the city, and was the secretary to Spon Street Ward Liberal Association. George was also a member of the Warwickshire Yeomanry. In the local Volunteer movement he was promoted to the rank of sergeant in 'B' Company. George was also the secretary of Radford Horticultural Society.

George, like many landlords at the time, brewed his own beer, and for this purpose kept a 5 foot high "copper" in the brew house behind the main building. One particular day, he filled the vat with 120 gallons of water to boil. At about midday his wife Elizabeth heard him cry out. She rushed to see what the problem was only to find her husband inside the vat, struggling to get out and screaming in agony.

It appears whilst standing on a stool to stir the contents he had fallen in head first. As his wife ran to help him he shouted "Oh Liz save me!" She helped him out as he muttered "It's my death blow". And so it was because even though his wife got him to the hospital by cab he was sinking deeply into shock. At the hospital Dr. H. Day said that George was practically scalded all over and he later died from shock.

The inquest was held at St. Mary's Hall and the verdict of accidental death was returned, George died 13th December 1899. He was 35 at the time of his death. Interred here also is Hannah Bale who died 29th September 1909, aged 81, Elizabeth Gascoyne who died 12th January 1939, aged 73, and William Thomas Gascoyne who died 3rd September 1965, aged 92. George's widow Elizabeth remarried becoming Elizabeth Gascoyne on marrying William. Hannah Bale is thought to be Elizabeth's mother. On the headstone there is the symbol of a sickle, which represents the reaping of a life, or for someone who has died young.

Grave 41 Sq 70.

EDMUND GABRIEL RICE.

Edmund Gabriel Rice was the only son of Dr Charles Rice and his wife Elsie. He was always referred to as Gabriel, and was a former pupil at Wolverhampton Grammar School.

Gabriel joined the Royal Navy Air Service in June 1917 and went on to receive training at Crystal Palace and Manton near Margate. He was sent to France and attained the rank of sub-lieutenant by the following December, staying on active service in France until March 1918. His service career was dramatically altered, however, due to an accident which occurred whilst on a scouting mission. Flying at a height of 18,000 feet, he fainted and did not regain consciousness until his aircraft had fallen to 4,000 feet. Fortunately, he was able to land his plane safely, but as a result of this accident he was invalided home.

He was made an instructor and sent to the air station at Redcar in Yorkshire on 29th April 1918. It was whilst there that he met with a fatal flying accident on 3rd May.

Gabriel was buried at London Road Cemetery with full military honours on 8th May. He was 18 years and 11 months old. Incidentally, Gabriel's nephew, the son of his sister, was the late Sir Nigel Hawthorne, famous stage and television actor who was born in Coventry. Some of this information was passed on to me by Gabriel's family, including his niece, Sheila, who was 84 years old at the time, and living in Cape Town, South Africa. At the time of his death, Gabriel's parents address in Coventry was Mansfield Villa, Binley Road, which is ironically now a doctor's surgery.

The headstone to this grave is quite impressive being of Portland stone topped with the out stretched eagle wings of the Royal Air Force. Underneath this a propeller is carved and either side of the stone are two straight columns. By the time of Gabriel's death, the Royal Flying Corps and the Royal Naval Air Service had amalgamated to form the Royal Air Force. This happened on 1st April 1918 - twenty eight days before he died. The full inscription reads:-

'LIEUTENANT EDMUND GABRIEL RICE BORN JUNE 3RD 1899

UNTO EACH MAN HIS HANDYWORK UNTO EACH HIS CROWN THE JUST FATE GIVES:
WHO SO TAKES THE WoRLdS LIFE ON HIM AND HIS OWN LAYS DoWN
HE, DYING SO LIVES.
SEEING DEATH HAS NO PART IN HIM. NO POWER

UPON HIS HEAD
HE HAS BOUGHT HIS ETERNITY WITH A LITTLE Help
AND IS NOT DEAD.

KNOWN AND UNKNOWN
HUMAN DIVINE.
SWEET HUMAN HAND AND LIPS AND EYES
DEAR HEAVENLY SON THAT CANST NOT DIE
AND MINE FOREVER MINE'.

The unusual mixture of upper and lower case letters in the inscription is transcribed as it is on the memorial. The first part of this inscription is taken from the poem by Swinburne- 'Super Flumina Babylonis'. The second part, starting with the words 'Known and unknown' is taken from Tennyson's elegy: 'In Memoriam'. Incidentally, this poem was a great favourite of Queen Victoria, who after the death of Prince Albert wrote that she was 'soothed and pleased' by it. In 1862, Victoria requested a meeting with Tennyson because she was so impressed by the poem, and when she met him again in 1883 she told him what a comfort it had been.

Gabriel's name appears on the roll of honour at Wolverhampton Grammar School to all former pupils who lost their lives in the Great War. It is called the Old Wulfrunians Roll of Honour, as former pupils of the School are referred to as 'Old Wulfrunians'.

Grave 42 Sq 34.

A picture of the burial service from the Coventry and Warwickshire Graphic.

ARTHUR CHARLES ROBINSON

Arthur Charles "Nat" Robinson was born in 1877, and by the age of 18 in 1895 became the goalkeeper for Singers FC. Nat was still with the club in 1898 when it changed its name to Coventry City FC. He then went on to join Small Heath in1899, and was with that club when it changed its name to Birmingham FC in 1905. Nat stayed three years, but in 1908 went to Chelsea FC for two seasons. In 1910, Nat returned to Coventry City FC and played his last game for the club on 27th March 1915, a 1-0 home win against Llanelli, in Southern League Division Two.

On Nat's retirement from football he became the licensee at the Old Ball Hotel, Walsgrave Road for two and half years. He then took over at the Old Red Horse Inn, Barras Green and this is where he would spend the rest of his life. Based at the Old Red Horse, Nat became a sports caterer, retaining connections with Highfield Road. He carried out the arrangements for functions there for a number of years.

Nat was also one of the promoters of an annual boxing tournament that was held in the city and in support of what was then called the Crippled Children's Guild.

Nat died on 15th May 1929, aged 52 having suffered with pneumonia for a couple of weeks. He was greatly mourned by all those who remembered him from his playing days and for his philanthropic work. He was also regarded as one of Coventry's most reliable authorities on the history of Singers FC and Coventry City FC.

Nat's funeral was attended by over a thousand people. Long before the cortège arrived at the Cemetery, many stood waiting by the road leading to the gates to pay their respects to this greatly admired all-round sportsman. Nat was also respected for philanthropic work as the Stoke Philanthropic Society was based at the Red Horse. Once the main funeral party passed through the gates a large group of members of the Stoke Philanthropic Society formed up to follow behind. Amongst the large gathering at the graveside were former team mates from his playing days, directors of Coventry City FC and the President and Vice-President of the Coventry Licensed Victuallers Association. At the graveside 125 wreaths were laid.

The grave has a black marble headstone and kerb set decorated with green chippings. In the centre is an urn engraved with the inscription:-

'ARTHUR.
FROM FRIENDS OF THE OLD RED HORSE.
GONE BUT NOT FORGOTTEN'.

Brewery records show that Florence, Nat's wife continued as licensee of the Old Red Horse Pub for a further 13 years, leaving in 1940. Florence died on 12th May 1960, aged 72. **Grave 8 Sq 61.**

The Old Red Horse Inn is still open today as a public house, unlike many other old pubs that seem to close for good, on a regular basis in these modern times.

The Old Red Horse Inn pictured in more recent times. Picture IW.

J.B. SHELTON M.B.E.

John Bailey Shelton, the son of a farm labourer was born on 19th March 1875, in Kirkby Woodhouse, a village between Nottingham and Mansfield. From the age of 11, he had spent his life working as a farm boy. Later in life, he was known for his way with horses, and perhaps these early years were the foundation of his love of the animal.

John came to Coventry as a young man of 22, in 1897. His first job when he arrived in the town was as a drayman for the London and North Western Railway at Coventry Station. It appears that he first went for an interview as an engine driver, but it became apparent to the person conducting the interview that John knew a lot more about handling horses than he ever would about driving a steam train! At this time anything that was delivered by train would be delivered across the town by horse drawn carts, hence the need for draymen.

John attended the Young People's Bible Class at Warwick Lane Chapel, and there he met Mary Catherine Aston. They married in the same Chapel on 12th August 1899 and they began married life together in a house in Cow Lane, eventually having two children: Bailey and Kathleen.

With a family to support, John became ambitious for a better living and made plans to start his own haulage business. By 1907, he had saved £100 to make a start in this venture. The family moved to premises in Little Park Street, which as well as providing accommodation for the family also had stabling for his horses.

His main haulage contract was with Bushills, an old and well-established Coventry firm that produced printed cardboard boxes and ribbon cards for the towns growing ribbon trade. Incidentally, Bushills was also based in Little Park Street. By the 1920s, John's business was thriving and he had six powerful and hardworking carthorses in its stables.

John was often referred to as JB and was known as a kind and thoughtful man. In 1923, he was elected to the Board of Guardians, thus being responsible for the well-being of the inmates of the Workhouse at the top of Gulson Road, in the building which had once been Whitefriars Monastery. For many years JB would walk there every Sunday with pockets full of small bags of sweets that would be distributed whilst chatting to each inmate in turn. Also on these visits he would take along pairs of glasses which he would buy from Woolworths for 6d a pair with the hope that anyone with faulty vision might be able to get some benefit from them. He remained on the board till 1930, and then became a member of the Social Welfare Committee which replaced it until 1948.

At the end of February 1927, at the age of 52, JB broke his leg. It was a complicated fracture, with four breaks in the leg: it was thought that he had been kicked by one of the horses. It was during his nine week stay in Coventry and Warwickshire Hospital that his interest in the history and archaeology of Coventry was first stimulated. For some time before his accident, JB had been reading the story of ancient Coventry, and with this break in his routine he was able to do more research. When discharged from hospital, and still on crutches, he would often make his way to the building site of the public house, the Hare and Squirrel. This was a short distance from his home in Much Park Street and JB became very interested in observing the contractor's trenches. He knew that in those trenches should be evidence of the monastic house of the Franciscan Friars or Greyfriars, which was built in around 1234. As time went on JB would revisit this site and others around the town when building work was undertaken, to build up a picture of the area and its buildings from the past. The extent of archaeology that was undertaken by JB over the years was immense and would go on to form the nucleus of the archaeology collection of the Herbert Art Gallery.

During the 1930s, JB wrote numerous articles in 'Austin's Monthly Magazine' detailing his findings. These articles are an incredible record of his work and as such, they helped people to work out where many streets and buildings had once been situated in Coventry.

In 1939, came the Second World War and on the night of 14th & 15th November 1940, the devastation of the Blitz was to effect JB's life as drastically as so many others that night. By now, both children had grown up, married and moved away, leaving JB and Mary living in Much Park Street. On the night of the Blitz, their house was gutted in the raid. A large portion of his considerable library was destroyed, with him only being able to save about forty books. JB, however, was soon to face a more difficult challenge. The stables containing his five horses had escaped damage, but in the early hours of the night, JB and his neighbour George Sheppard, concerned with the safety of the animals, decided to move the horses. With a great deal of effort, the two of them managed to move them all into the garden where they were able to tether them to a tree. It's hard for us to imagine the magnitude of this event and the courage of the two men. Moving large, frightened animals during a night-time of fire and explosions would not be something many people would attempt. For this act of bravery, John and George were later awarded the Queen Victoria medal of the RSPCA.   Life was never to be the same for JB, however, as Mary had been badly injured during the raid and although she partially recovered, she was never fully well again and died in 1946. JB published a small book in 1950, ten years after the raid, entitled: 'A Night in Little Park Street', recounting the events of that evening.

JB continued to live in the remains of the house, making use of two caravans in the yard. He set up a display in the house calling it the Benedictine

Museum where he showed his archaeological collection of pots, knives, leather work, horseshoes etc.

Towards the end of the war, in March 1945, the City council appointed him to the post of City Chamberlain of Coventry, an honour that he valued very highly. This had been an office of the city council since 1269, and was held by two men each year. His main duty was to be the official guide to visitors to St Mary's Hall, and he received an honorarium of 100 guineas a year. His presence there meant that he met many people interested in Coventry's history. He also wrote many pieces for schools on the history of their areas, and gave evening lectures to local groups and organisations.

After living in the caravans for some time, the Council found him a cottage at the top of Priory Street, the address being 7, St Michael's Churchyard. This meant that he would watch the early stages of the construction of the new Coventry Cathedral.

In 1956 for his many years of public service and dedication to history and archaeology he was awarded the M.B.E. and collected it from Buckingham Palace with his proud daughter and granddaughter.

On the 22nd November 1958, JB was on his way to read the newspaper to a blind friend which was something he did every day. While crossing the road at the top of Green Lane he was knocked down by a motorbike and taken to Coventry and Warwickshire Hospital with severe injuries. Sadly, John passed away a week later. He was aged 83.

John Bailey Shelton was a life-long Methodist and was a trustee of Central Hall for many years, and so this was where his funeral service took place, followed by interment at the cemetery. He was buried with his wife Mary who, as mentioned earlier had died on 17th January 1946, aged 68. The headstone on the grave of JB and Mary presents a puzzle. Their names are inscribed on the kerb set on either side of the grave, not on the headstone. The headstone is inscribed with the names of Richard Gribble, died 3rd January 1930 and Edith Gribble, died on 5th October, 1946, aged 68. By searching through the census records, it has been found that Edith's father was a drayman by profession, and possibly knew or worked for JB Incidentally, a few years after the death of Richard Gribble, Edith was listed as living with the Sheltons.

A short distance to the right of this grave is a grave with a white headstone and kerb set. Inscribed on the headstone are the names Annie Letitia Sheppard, died on 6th January 1930, aged 50, and George Henry, died 30th July 1951, aged 65. This is the same George Sheppard who on that fateful night in November 1940 helped JB move the five horses to safety. George was a veteran of the First World War and worked as a drayman for a local brewery which must have helped when moving the horses that night.

John Bailey Shelton is now remembered in several locations in Coventry: Shelton Square, John Shelton Primary School, in Briscoe Road and John Shelton Drive, Holbrooks. The young lad who first set foot in Coventry in 1897 has certainly left his mark on the City, a City with a history of which he become very proud and passionate.

John Shelton's archaeological methods were in later years criticised by some people because he didn't remove items in chronological order as you would today, losing the time-scale knowledge contained in the layers of soil. However, it is more than likely that the objects found would have been lost forever had John not rescued them. And on that basis he is regarded by many as a pioneer of 'rescue archaeology'.

Grave 25 Sq 106.

REVEREND JOHN SIBREE

The Reverend John Sibree was described by some as a raging individualist in a time when his profession abounded with them. In 1820 he became minister to the Congregation at Vicar Lane Chapel, after attending Hoxton College, London. John Sibree's father was an Independent Minister of Frome, and John's other brothers Peter and James became ministers. It is said John Sibree had a gift of attracting publicity, perhaps even for 'self dramatisation'!

In 1821 Reverend Sibree was called to visit a criminal in Coventry jail. The man Edward Bradshaw was under sentence of death for burglary at the Punch Bowl Public House in Spon End, where he was accused of cutting and wounding a Mr Lines who had come to the aid of the landlord Mr Bobbet. On the day of execution, he accompanied the accused and a police officer, atop the coffin as it was taken through the streets of Coventry to Whitley Common which was the place of execution. Large crowds gathered at the gallows. On the Sunday after the execution Reverend Sibree planned to preach a sermon at Vicar Lane Chapel but the Chapel proved too small. Those in attendance were moved to Warwick Row where he addressed the crowd from a balcony of a nearby house. The crowd by now had gathered on Greyfriars Green and had swelled to between 6,000 and 7,000.

His views were advanced for the time as he was an opponent of capital punishment. It is said that the Reverend Sibree frequently thundered against Anglicanism and capital punishment from the pulpit of Vicar Lane Chapel. There is no doubt that one would have little chance of drifting off for a nap in one of his services!

The Sibrees were said to be cultured, well-educated people. His son taught Greek to Mary Ann Evans (George Eliot). His daughter Mary became the wife of John Cash of J & J Cash fame. Sibree was also a friend of Francis Franklin, minister of Cow Lane Baptist Church, and he preached his funeral oration.

Reverend Sibree's funeral cortege arrived at the Cemetery on Thursday 5th April at 12 noon. The procession through the Cemetery to the Chapel was led by a body of over 16 ministers from Coventry and neighbouring towns, and was joined by Reverend Canon Baynes. The Chapel was crowded and the Reverend

E.H.Delf delivered an address in which he said 'of our departed and reverend friend we may say thou art gone to thy grave in full age, as a shock of corn cometh in his season.' Reverend Sibree had died quite suddenly even though he was advanced in age and he still preached regularly. However when he was close to death he had said to his wife 'I am going to take possession of my inheritance.' John Sibree was the oldest minister in Coventry when he died, and quite possibly in the whole country. Shortly after his death this piece appeared in the local press:-

'IN MEMORIAM
THE REV. JOHN SIBREE
DIED ON EASTER EVE, MARCH 31, 1877 IN HIS 82ND YEAR.
He sleeps: the sire of fourscore years and more
Is garner'd as a ripened shock of corn;
God's reapers took him on the eve before
The Saviour's glorious resurrection morn.
In life he boldly fought the fight of faith,
And now hath sheathed the victor's well worn sword—
He sweetly sleeps; the faithful unto death,
With blessed dead departed in the Lord.'

Although the stonework is quite weather beaten, a shock of corn is visible at the top of the memorial on the grave, with the inscription underneath which reads:-

'AS A SHOCK OF CORN FULLY RIPE.'

Reverend Sibree died 31st March 1877 aged 81. Also interred here are his wife Charlotte who died 28th September 1865 aged 81, and his second wife Louisa who died 20th November 1904, aged 76. **Grave 6 Sq 82.**

Some citizens of Coventry may remember Sibree Hall at the rear of Warwick Road Congregational Church, and Sibree Road which is on the Stonebridge Industrial Estate in Baginton near Coventry.

GEORGE SINGER

George Singer was born in Kingston, Dorset on 26th January 1847, the son of a bailiff also called George, who is said to have been of Scottish descent.

He served an apprenticeship with John Penn and Sons, the marine engineers of Lewisham, where James Starley had once worked as a gardener. In 1869, George moved to Coventry to join The Coventry Machinists Company which was run by James Starley. George would have known James Starley, Josiah Turner, and William Hillman: all pioneers in the early cycle industry, before they all came to Coventry to make their mark.

George soon rose to the rank of foreman at Coventry Machinists. On 15th January 1873, he married Eliza Stringer from nearby Kenilworth at Vicar Lane Chapel, Coventry. He left Coventry Machinists in the following year. In 1875, at the age of 28, he joined in partnership with his brother-in-law James Charles Stringer and formed Singer and Co with a capital of £300. The first cycle made by the new company was called the Challenge followed by the Racing Challenge and the Special Challenge and these were all of the Penny Farthing type. Following success in cycle manufacturing and motorcycle manufacturing the first Singer car went on sale in 1905.

George was keen for all his employees to enjoy sports and other social activities. The company formed cycle, cricket and football clubs. The cricket and football teams played against other local companies, with some success. But the football team went on to much greater things. Founded in 1883, they were called Singers FC and their first president was George Singer. The nickname for the team was the Vocalists. Until 1887, only employees of Singer and Co were allowed to play. In 1894, the team joined the Birmingham League and in 1898 the club changed its name to Coventry City FC, joining the Football League in 1919.

George was also Mayor of Coventry for three years in succession 1891, 1892, and 1893.

George died on Monday 3rd January 1909, aged 61, at his residence Coundon Court, which has since become a secondary school of the same name.

Eliza is also interred here. She had left Coventry some time after George had died and according to her obituary had died at Harley House, Regent's Park,

London. She died 3rd March 1918, aged 73. Eliza's funeral took place at the Cemetery after her coffin was conveyed from London by hearse. The hearse was met at the Cemetery gates by mourners, with the Rev Frank Taylor, vicar of Walsgrave-on-Sowe conducting the burial service. As well as family members present, there were many local business people and council members who still remembered the support Eliza had given George during his three terms in office as mayor of Coventry.

This particular monument is one of the finest funerary monuments within the Cemetery. The decoration is very detailed, consisting of a cross adorned with passion flowers, representing, of course, the passion of Christ.

Grave 1 Sq 49.

Incidentally, James Stringer, George's business partner is buried near to George and Eliza. He died 1st November 1915, aged 52.

In 2011, a bench was installed near George's grave. At present, this bench is the only one in this part of the Cemetery. Its position makes it the ideal place to sit and appreciate the trees, monuments, wildlife and stillness so near the city centre. On a small brass plate reads the inscription:-

**'IN MEMORY OF GEORGE SINGER VEHICLE MANUFACTURER
AND THREE TIMES MAYOR OF COVENTRY
THIS BENCH WAS DONATED BY FRIENDS OF LONDON ROAD
AND SINGER ENTHUSIASTS 25/01/2011.'**

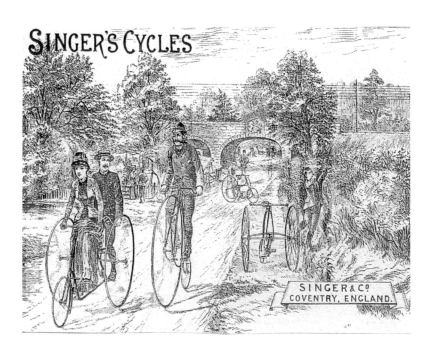

FRANCIS SKIDMORE

Francis Alfred Skidmore or 'Skidmore of Coventry' as he became known was one of the best art metalworkers in the country during the Victorian period.

Born in Birmingham in 1817, his father was a jeweller who moved with his family to Coventry in 1822. Young Francis was apprenticed to his father in the jewellery and metalwork trade. Skidmore's earliest works are thought to be pieces of church plate in around 1845. They included a chalice for St Giles' Church, Exhall and another for the church of St John the Baptist in Coventry. In 1851, Skidmore displayed some beautiful pieces of church plate at the Great Exhibition in the Crystal Palace. This was to make him an artist of national importance and as a result, he started commissions in Coventry and further afield. The first example of his church screen work was completed in 1852, in the church of St Mary's Cubbington, a small village near Leamington. By 1853, Francis had set up his own business in West Orchard and employed 24 people.

As the Gothic revival grew within the Church of England in the 1840s, so did Skidmore's reputation. He was influenced by this movement and this can be seen in much of his work. This led to many commissions from leading architects of the day. He also became interested in the development of gas lighting, and in 1850 created a scheme for St Mary's Hall, in 1851 he did the same for St Michael's, and in 1856 created a similar scheme for Holy Trinity, along with the altar fender which can still be seen today. In 1859, he moved to larger premises in Alma Street, and by 1865 employed 74 men and 54 boys, making it one of the largest factories in Coventry at that time. These same premises were later taken over by the Singer Cycle Company.

His most productive partnership was with Sir George Gilbert Scott. The two men had first met when Scott was restoring several churches in Coventry in the 1850s. The firm worked on many church choir screens. The most well known was the Hereford Screen, in Hereford Cathedral measuring 36ft wide and 34ft tall. It was removed from the Cathedral in 1967 and put into storage by the Herbert Art Gallery, with the intention of including it in a new industrial museum but this never happened and it was to remain in crates until 1984. The Hereford Screen was eventually taken on by the Victoria and Albert Museum in London. £750,000 was raised to restore it and it was finally unveiled in May 2001, where it is on permanent display.

Skidmore was at his most productive in the 1860s and 1870s and his innovative iron, brass and silverwork won him great acclaim and prestigious commissions like the Albert Memorial and the Midland Railway Hotel at St Pancras Station, London. An interesting story told at the time concerns the metal work made for the Albert Memorial. It was said that as it grew taller in the yard in Alma Street, the ornate metalwork could be seen rising from behind the fence.

Another choir screen was made and installed in Lichfield Cathedral. It is still there today and it is well worth a visit to the cathedral in order to appreciate this stunning work in the place for which it was designed.

Francis was a perfectionist and this was his downfall. He often threw away work which he considered less than perfect and naturally, this lost him a lot of money. He sold his Coventry business in 1872 and set up a smaller concern in Meriden, which he called Skidmore's Art Metal Works. It was situated in the Manor House which is now the Manor Hotel. In 1881, he was employing 11 men and 12 boys, but in the late 1880s, the company was taken over by Winfields of Birmingham.

In later life, Skidmore was not as well off financially as he should have been. He moved to Eagle Street Coventry, and spent his later years receiving the Freeman's Seniority Pension. It is said he spent most of his time visiting Holy Trinity and St Michael's Church to look at his work. By now his eyesight was failing, and he had been disabled after he had been knocked down by a horse and carriage.

Francis Skidmore played an important part in the history of English decorative metalwork and when he died his obituary mentioned that there were examples of his work in 22 cathedrals, 300 parish churches and 20 town halls and public buildings.

Francis Skidmore died in November 1896, aged 79. His wife Emma died in May 1901, aged 70. Also buried in this plot are the parents of Francis: his mother Flora, died 3rd January 1849, aged 68, while his father, also called Francis died 13th January 1860, aged 79. Another Francis is buried in this plot: Francis Sidney Skidmore, Francis and Emma's son who died in March 1911, aged 55. **Grave 15 Sq 27.**

DAVID SPENCER

David Spencer was born on November 19th 1805, in Little Heath Foleshill, and was the son of a ribbon manufacturer, William Spencer. David was educated at private schools in the parish. On leaving school he was apprenticed to William Browett, a general draper.

After serving the full term of 7 years of his apprenticeship, David entered the trade on his own on the 4th May 1828, as a general draper in Hay Lane with a capital of £30. David was only 22 years of age at the time.

David excelled in business and became well-known for his good heartedness and kind nature. He was not only known as a shopkeeper but was also a 'genial and jocular' man. It was said that a child sent for a pennyworth of thread was given the same courtesy as an adult requiring a large parcel of goods. In his shop he developed the woollen department in such a way that he built up a monopoly in this area. He eventually discarded general drapery to concentrate on the sale of carpets. Sometime later this part of the business was transferred to two of his long standing members of staff, John Anslow and Richard Roden.

Over the years, David became known for his philanthropic ways. He was a great supporter of the church and was instrumental in helping people free themselves from debt, whatever their religious beliefs. David made considerable donations to the Coventry and Warwickshire Hospital, in addition to the annual subscriptions he was expected to pay as a supporter of the hospital. He also donated £250 to St Michael's restoration fund, but it is his connection with Spencer recreation grounds and the Technical Institute that he was best remembered for. At that time, a portion of Stivichale Common known as Top Green had been designated by the City Council as an area to be used for cricket, football and other sports and £70 had been spent to level it. It was an area of about four acres and David often walked there and thought it would be a great spot for a recreation ground, if the area could be increased.

Not all the owners of the surrounding land were keen to sell their land in order to increase the size of the proposed park. One of the owners who was happy to sell was Robert Dalton, a local land owner and councillor. Dalton Road, at the top of the park was later named after him. Due to the fact that other land owners would not sell, David approached the trustees of King Henry VIII Grammar School. The school owned a meadow of seven acres, which was surplus to requirements. The school trustees were happy to sell the land as the proceeds could then be used to finance the start of building work on the new school much earlier than had been expected. Once this was agreed, David handed an additional cheque for £4,000 to the Mayor, Alderman Scampton saying if this was not enough to finish the work he would reimburse the Corporation any extra that might be needed. It has to be remembered that this sum of money was considerable in Victorian times. The park was opened by Mayor Albert Samuel Tomson on the 11th October 1883. We know it today as Spencer Park.

In 1887, David helped establish the Technical Institute by offering the committee a plot of land with buildings in Earl Street, and remarked that it had always been his habit to start things on a small scale and see them develop. This gift was to the value of £2,000 or more, with another £500 towards working expenses.

In May the following year 1888, David was struck with an 'attack of paralysis' from which he was not to recover. David Spencer died 9th June, aged 83, at his residence, 22 Warwick Row. It was almost a year after the death of his beloved wife Tabitha who had died on 18th July 1887. Also interred here is Tabitha's niece Tabitha, who died 24th April 1918, aged 71, and her husband Arthur Massey Spencer who died 11th March 1923, aged 78. Unusually, Arthur's surname is also Spencer because he had changed it by deed poll some years earlier.

When David Spencer's will was read, he had left family and friends the sum of £75,000 and also left in trust the sum of £20,000 to be used for charitable causes within the city.

Grave 1 Sq 65.

Flowers at the grave on the day of the funeral.

WILLIE STANLEY

Willie Stanley was born in Birmingham on the 12th February 1861. At the time, his parents, Amelia and Enoch, were living in Great Colmore Street, in the centre of Birmingham. Shortly after Willie was born the family moved back to Wolverhampton, which was where Willie's parents had originally come from.Willie's father died in December 1863, aged 31. By April 1865, Amelia had married a James Bowers and in December of the same year they had a son, George.

By 1881, the Bowers family, which included Willie, were living at 26, Pountney Street, in the Blakenhall district of Wolverhampton. Willie was nineteen and working as a fitter and turner.

Later in 1881, Willie moved to Coventry taking up a position at the Singer Cycle works. In October of the following year, the rest of the Bowers family arrived in Coventry. George Bowers was also able to find employment at Singers with his half-brother.

Willie and George had always been keen footballers since they were at school, and when the Singer Football Club was formed at the Lord Aylesford Inn, Hillfields on Monday 13th August 1883, it was founded by Willie, who became the club's secretary. Also present at the formation of the club were George Bowers, along with Henry Banks, Henry Hathaway, Samuel Heath, Francis Moseley, Andrew Poole and Herbert Turner, who all became founder players. All members of the team at that time were Singer's employees based at Alma Street. The very first match played by Singers was against Coventry Association, with Coventry winning 9-0. As mentioned elsewhere in this book Singers Football Club would eventually become Coventry City Football Club in 1898.

1883 seems to have been quite eventful because on 30th December, Willie married his childhood sweetheart Sarah Bailey at Saint James's Parish Church, Wolverhampton. Willie and Sarah started married life at 11 Vine Street, Hillfields, Coventry. They went on to have three children, a son and two daughters.

Willie and his family, however, left Coventry in early 1886, when he started his own business as an agent, manufacturing, retailing and repairing bicycles at Stafford Street, Walsall. This move put an end to Willie's role as secretary of Singer's Football Club. That position was taken on by Henry Hathaway, one of the founder members. Willie was qualified as a master bicycle builder and initially his bicycle shop was a success. By 1891, he became wealthy enough to employ a domestic servant at his home. However things changed dramatically and in late 1893 or early 1894 Willie was declared bankrupt. Trade was particularly fierce around this time with many people in the bicycle trade all after the same customers.

The family returned to Coventry and lived at 22 Oxford Street, Hillfields. The loss of the business must have been a bitter blow to Willie, but sadly, worse was to come. Sarah caught influenza, and within days this developed into bronchial-pneumonia. Two days later, on 2nd March 1895, Sarah had died. She was 30 years of age.

In May 1896, Willie married again, to Agnes Evans, at Saint Mary and Saint Benedict's Roman Catholic Church in Raglan Street, Hillfields. Agnes was originally from Walsall and the family moved back there in 1897. Willie's occupation is described at this time as 'engine fitter' which means he might have gained employment in the motor cycle industry. By 1901, the family were living back in Coventry in Days Lane. Willie's brother ran his own cycle business, Stanley's Bicycle Company in Days Lane, so he may have moved here to be near his brother and possibly worked for him. By 1905 the Stanley family was living in Alma Street, with Willie by then working as a machine tool maker. It is thought that he worked for the Humber works in Lower Ford Street. In 1910 the Stanley family were now living at 27, Charterhouse Road, in the Stoke area and near the newly opened Humber factory on Folly Lane, later known as Humber Road. In their new home Willie and Agnes had another three children.

Willie died at home on 13th June, 1933, aged 72 and Agnes died on 5th March, 1956, aged 84. Also buried in this plot are two of their children. Their daughter Edith Titmus died in 1938, aged 27 and their son Frank Stanley died in 1951, aged 49. Also, Thomas Varley, who died in 1936, aged 50 is recorded as being buried in this plot, but it is not certain who Thomas is, or what connects him to the family. **Grave 75 Sq 118.**

GEORGE BOWERS

What became of Willie's half-brother and co-founder player of Singers Football Club George Bowers? He seems to have led a more simple life than Willie. George played for Singers for five years, most of the time playing on the right wing. Retiring from the playing staff in 1888, he still stayed as a member of the club and would sometimes take on the role of linesman. George would also occasionally play Rugby Union for Singers RFC. George married Harriet Preedy on 4th September 1887, at All Saints Church, Far Gosford Street. They did not have any children. In 1901,

George was still employed as a bicycle machinist, but surprisingly was also a fried fish seller, with his shop being close to the Greyhound Inn in Little Park Street. He probably learnt this particular trade from his father who had himself worked as a fried fish seller. George died on 8th March 1951, aged 85. Harriett died on 13th March 1932, as a result of a tragic accident in which she was knocked down by a motor cycle when crossing the road. When George and Harriett were buried, they joined George's parents, his mother Amelia who died in 1907, aged 75 and his father James who died in 1908, aged 69. **Grave 209 Sq 117.**

All of this information comes courtesy of Lionel Bird, who over a great number of years has done meticulous research into the history of Singers Football Club. Whilst researching, Lionel discovered that both Willie and George were buried in London Road Cemetery and he was saddened to find that neither grave had a headstone or marker of any kind. He started a public appeal fund in January 2007, to raise the funds to erect headstones for these two pioneers in Coventry's football history. A major donation was received from Coventry City Football Club, also members of Coventry City Supporters Club, with other major donations from the Sky Blue Trust and Cov Support Website. £2,055 in total was collected in just three months. The new headstones were erected by April 2008, and on Friday the 4th April a special service took place at the Cemetery. Approximately forty descendants of Willie Stanley gathered at his graveside as the headstone was blessed in a ceremony performed by Father Bob Wright of Saint John Fisher's Roman Catholic Church. The new headstone for George Bowers, which is nearby, was also blessed. The first part of the inscription on Willie' headstone reads:-

'IN MEMORY
OF
WILLIE STANLEY
Founder of Singers F.C. 1883
(Coventry City F.C. 1898)'

The first part of George's headstone reads:-

'IN MEMORY
OF
GEORGE EDWARD
BOWERS
Founder Player Of
Singers F.C. 1883'

On Tuesday 13th August 2013, a small memorial service was held at the grave of Willie Stanley, to mark 130th anniversary of the formation of Singers FC.

Among the guests were Willie's great granddaughters, Enid Frapwell and Ann William, along with great grandson Ian Devoy. A small posy of pink, navy blue and white flowers was laid at the grave. These colours represented the first known Coventry City playing kit and the Singer Company.

The grave of Willie Stanley, 18th August 2013. Picture IW.

JAMES STARLEY

James Starley was born at Woodbine Cottage, Albourne, Sussex, 21ˢᵗ April 1830; he was the fourth of five children to Daniel a farmer and his wife Ann. The young James started work for his father at the age of 11 but at the age of 16 James had a dispute with his father and left for London.

He first found work at Wilmot and Chaudey's Nursery in Lewisham. He then worked for John Penn and Sons, marine engineers, as an under gardener at their residence, the Cedars. Part of young James's duties was to wheel John Penn II in his bath chair to the factory in the mornings as Mr Penn suffered from a form of paralysis.

While at the factory James would sneak into the workshops and gain knowledge of engineering methods, and started to invent small gadgets such as an adjustable candlestick. He also cleaned watches and repaired pianos.

A young sewing maid who worked at the Cedars named Jane Todd caught the eye of James as he went about his duties. In time their friendship blossomed into romance, and in 1853, Jane and James were married in the Union Chapel Lewisham.

In his spare time, James took on the task of trying to repair a sewing machine that belonged to the wife of John Penn. He stripped it down and reassembled it so that it worked perfectly. John Penn was so impressed with this that he went to his friend Josiah Turner who was manager of the company that produced the sewing machine, Newton and Wilson and Co of Holborn. On Mr Penn's insistence James was employed by Mr Turner in 1859. Mr Turner would go on to pay for James's early patents, and drawings of improvements that he came up with for the company's sewing machines.

In May 1861, he left London with Josiah Turner and an American called Salisbury and came to Coventry to make sewing machines. A firm was set up called the Coventry Sewing Machine Company. It was based in King Street, in the district of Cheylesmore. The first machines produced were called, 'The European', 'Godiva', 'Express' and 'Swiftsure'.

In the November of 1868, a nephew of Mr Turner's, Rowley B. Turner, returned from Paris with an iron-tyred wooden bone-shaker, an early type of bicycle. James could see immediately the potential in this machine, and straight away set about improving it until he came up with what became known as the Velocipede. By 1869 they were receiving large orders and it was around this time that the company became the Coventry Machinists Company Ltd.

James worked with William Hillman, someone he had known and worked with at Penn's in London. Together they developed a penny-farthing type of bicycle called the Ariel, and took out a patent for this in 1870. This was an early light weight machine, constructed completely of metal, and the first to have tension wheels with spokes that would tighten to increase rigidity.

In 1877, James made a four wheeled cycle for two riders called the Comfortable Sociable and it was while producing this machine that he invented the differential gear which is still found in every car today in some type of form!

When William Hillman went on to form a company on his own, called Hillman, Herbert and Cooper, James formed a company called Starley Brothers. James's three sons became involved in the business headed by his eldest, William.

One person who became a fan of the exciting machines produced by Starley Brothers was Queen Victoria herself, and this resulted in James presenting her with two Salvo Quad Tricycle machines at Osborne House, Isle of Wight.

Unfortunately, by now James knew he was an ill man, and that he was suffering from liver cancer. He impressed everyone by the stoical way that he dealt with his illness, and still carried on working, when he had the energy to do so. James Starley died 17th June 1881, at his home in Upper Well Street. He was aged 51. His death was announced not only in the local Coventry press but also in the London press, so well respected was this inventive and creative man.

In November 1884, the Starley Memorial was erected by the citizens of Coventry. It was erected in Queen's Grove but it was moved in 1922 when road widening took place at the top of Greyfriars Green. Queen's Grove disappeared when the ring road was constructed in the mid-1960s and early 1970s. The portrait of James carved on this memorial is the same as the one on the memorial seen on his grave.

Soon after the memorial at Queen's Grove was first erected a strange incident took place on the small piece of green which enclosed it. A cyclist alighted in front of the memorial and began to take his bicycle apart. A crowd gathered as he proceeded to reverently lay each part of the bicycle on the steps of the plinth as an offering, as it were, at the shrine of a genius that many refer to as the 'Father of the Bicycle'.

   Interred here also are James's wife Jane who died 10th September 1900, aged 74. Her address at the time was 16, Starley Road, named of course in honour of her famous husband. Apparently Jane quite liked being Mrs Starley of Starley Road!
One of their sons, also called James is buried here. He died 18th April 1942, aged 89.
Grave 4 Sq 29.

The Starley Memorial, shown in its original Queen's Grove location.

JOHN KEMP STARLEY

John Kemp Starley was born in Walthamstow on Christmas Eve, 1854. His father, also called John, was the brother of James Starley, the 'father of the cycle industry'.

Young John first came to Coventry in 1872, at the age of 18 to work for his uncle at the suggestion of his father, who had noticed his son's enthusiasm for anything mechanical. John moved in with his uncle and family who, at the time were living in Upper Well Street. His uncle James kept a workshop at the house, where he would work on prototypes of machines before going into production. This gave John a great opportunity to quickly learn the workings of the cycles as they developed.

John very quickly settled into life with his uncle, aunt and cousins in Coventry and soon began to make his own circle of friends. Most of these new friends were members of the West Orchard Chapel, which he had begun to attend regularly. One of these new friends was Abigail Statham, daughter of City Councillor and manufacturer George Statham.

By August 1876, John and Abigail were married at the West Orchard Chapel. John's sister Annie, and Abigail's father were witnesses. Members from both families were present, and an impressive wedding breakfast was held at the home of the bride's parents. John was 22, and Abigail just 19. The bride's father had a reputation for being difficult and there was some surprise when he gave his blessing to the union, considering how young his daughter was. It has been surmised that the groom's Uncle James may have put in a good word for his nephew, bearing in mind that James Starley was, by then, a well-respected figure and businessman in the town.

After about five years under the watchful eye of his uncle, John was found a position with Haynes and Jeffries. This company had done various types of work for James Starley at different times, and was now building his bicycles and tricycles under license. However, John did not stay with Haynes and Jeffries for long. He was ambitious and wanted to set up a business on his own. This was a difficult decision to make as he was still young and had a growing family to support. He must have had a great deal of conviction to pursue his career.

In 1878, John set up on his own to produce cycles and he was joined in partnership by a William Sutton. From then on the company was known as Starley and Sutton. Their first bicycle was called the 'Meteor' but it was his next machine that was to set him on the road to success. It is well documented that John Kemp

Starley was the inventor of the first safety cycle with the diamond shaped frame on which all bicycles are based, even today. This cycle was known as the 'Rover' and was the first to incorporate the newly invented pneumatic tyre from J.B. Dunlop.

John's main hobby was inevitably cycling, but away from this his other passion was shooting. He was said to be never happier than when he was tramping over the moors with a party of friends. He was also a councillor on Coventry Council for several years, and the president of the local Y.M.C.A.

In 1886, William Sutton retired and from that time on the company was known as J.K. Starley & Co, Limited. In 1896, John sold the company for the sum of £150,000. So highly principled was John in all his dealings that he actually refused a much higher offer. At this time the company was renamed the Rover Cycle Company Limited.

While all this was happening in John's business world, his domestic arrangements were also changing. When he and Abigail had first married they moved to Hertford Place, but as their fortunes changed they were able to consider something on a much grander scale. Barr's Hill House was purchased as the family home at sometime in the late 1890s, but it is thought that John rented the property for some years before that time. The property was purchased for £2,500 and included four acres of garden. John set about some internal alterations, the study was furnished in a Chinese style and he also made the addition of a gun room. A rather grand conservatory was added at around the same time.

On Tuesday, 16th August 1898, a great tragedy befell John and Abigail. Arthur their youngest son drowned in a boating accident while holidaying with his father and brother's Frank and Bert, in Barmouth, North Wales. The Starleys had been staying at Brynmynach Castle on the Harlech Road since late July; Abigail had returned to Coventry the previous week and planned to return the next day. John had gone out shooting for the day near Bala. The three boys remained at the house, and went out boating in the early afternoon. They had not long pushed off when they found themselves in the estuary and shortly after, the small craft sank, throwing Arthur into the water. He could swim a little and it was thought he would make it to the bank but he suddenly sank beneath the water. The other two boys were not out of danger either. Their cries for help alerted a boatman and they were both saved. Arthur's body was recovered at 4:30 pm. He was 16 years of age. John received the sad information at Bala, and quickly wired a telegram to his close friend, Reverend George Bainton, asking him to break the news to Abigail. Another telegram had been sent to Coventry to Abigail's father, and it was he who reached Barr's Hill House first with the sad news.

The next day an inquest was held in Barmouth and the jury returned a verdict of accidental death. Arthur's body was brought back to Coventry arriving at Barr's Hill House early on the Thursday. The funeral was held the following day. Before the coffin left the house, a short service was conducted by the Reverend Bainton. The cortege arrived at the cemetery just after 3:00pm and understandably this sad event drew a large amount of people to the Chapel and graveside.

Reverend Bainton delivered a very personal service at the Chapel. Here are some quotes from that service: "It is one of the greatest mysteries of life why a child dies before the father, a mystery to be solved only in the day when passing ourselves through the gateway of eternal life." Also "It has been my privilege to know Arthur Starley almost his whole life long, and to know him intimately. He was a bright, spirited happy hearted boy." A memorial service was delivered the following Sunday by Reverend Bainton at West Orchard Chapel and this was attended by John and Abigail with older members of the family. The Reverend Bainton's brother, as organist that day, played Chopin's Funeral March and finished with 'I Know my Redeemer Liveth' from Handel's Messiah.

John had worshipped at West Orchard Chapel since coming to Coventry and as mentioned earlier, married Abigail there. John was never afraid to show his strong Christian beliefs, and in spite of this, he continued to be a shrewd businessman.

John was suffering from gall stones, but his heart was said to be too weak for doctors to perform an operation. As a result of this John Kemp Starley died on the morning of Tuesday October 29th 1901, at the age of 46.

The funeral service was also taken by Reverend George Bainton, who was now a very close friend of John and his family. The cortege left Barr's Hill House at 11 o'clock on its journey to West Orchard Chapel, where the first part of the service was conducted. The route to the cemetery brought traffic to a standstill due to the size of the crowds of people gathering in the streets.

Floral tributes laid at the grave of J.K.Starley, November 2nd, 1901

It was reported that twenty thousand people had gathered at the cemetery. The vault that had first been created for his youngest son Arthur was reopened for the interment. A personal and touching tribute from Reverend Bainton followed. Speaking with obvious emotion he said "I have a very painful duty to perform in speaking to you this morning - a few simple words touching the great sorrow that has brought us here today." He then went onto say: "For eighteen years past Mr Starley has been my closest friend. He has made me his confident in almost all things, and we have talked together of each other's troubles, we have rejoiced together over each other's joys. No minister could have had a more confiding and generous companion in home and church." The funeral party included eight coaches to convey the mourners. The bearers consisted of eight servants of the Starley family, their period of service ranging from 18 to 25 years. The wreaths and tributes had amongst them one representing an open Bible from the members of the Y.M.C.A. Violets were used to form the words "Thy will be done."

Abigail outlived John by another 36 years and she died in 1937, aged 81, whilst living at 59, Beauchamp Avenue, Leamington Spa.

John and Abigail had 10 children in total and four of them are interred with their parents. As well as poor unfortunate Arthur, Bertram, also known as Bert, is buried here. He was one of the brothers who were with Arthur on that fateful boat trip. Bert died in 1949, aged 65. Also here is John Kemp Junior who died in 1941 aged 65. His first wife, Lillian is buried nearby. She died in 1901, at the age of 22. A third John Kemp Starley is also buried in the family vault. He was the son of John

Kemp Junior, from his second marriage. He died in 1972, aged 64, and had been living in Leamington Spa where many of his family lived by this time.

Barr's Hill House was brought by the City Council in 1907, to become a girls' school. Substantial extensions and alterations took place making the building almost twice the size. As time went on other buildings were added in the grounds, taking up the once stunning gardens. The original house was finally demolished and the site is now used as a car park for Barr's Hill School.

The Rover Company went on to produce motorcycles and in 1904, three years after John had died, they started to produce motorcars. This is the very same Rover name which has such a long association with the British motor industry.

John's brother, Richard and sister- in-law Mary are buried directly to the right of this vault. Richard appears to have been the owner of a great deal of property in and around the city. Richard died 3rd December 1908, aged 48. At the time of his death his address is recorded as being 20, Chester Street. Mary died 8th February 1935, aged 73 and she was still living in Chester Street when she died.
Grave 5 Sq 89.

The funeral cortege for J.K.Starley makes its way through Broadgate.

Crowds gather in Braodgate for J.K.Starley's cortege

THOMAS STEVENS

Thomas Stevens was born in 1828 in Foleshill which at the time was a village near Coventry. The son of a weaver of humble circumstances, Thomas was one of seven children, four sons and three daughters. In his youth he worked for Messrs Pears and Franklin as a ribbon-weaver, where he mastered all areas of the textile industry. By 1854, he had started his own weaving business at his home in Queens Street, Coventry. Soon after this however, with the repeal of the tax on imported ribbons and silks, the trade for these items almost vanished.

Thomas came up with the idea of manufacturing multicoloured bookmarks and other items such as pictures of famous people, landscapes, buildings etc. By 1875 he had built the Stevengraph Works in Cox Street, and had developed his weaving process so that it became known as a fine art. He took out many patents for his inventions and improvements in the industry, and was awarded over 30 medals, prizes, and diplomas.

In time, Thomas would take a loom to various exhibitions, including Crystal Palace, where he would demonstrate the process of weaving Stevengraphs, and then sell the woven bookmarks and pictures to the watching public. This explains why his work includes not only views of Coventry and nearby places such as Stoneleigh Abbey, but also historical scenes, views of the interior of the Crystal Palace and even bookmarks of Joseph Paxton himself!

Later on in life Thomas moved to London, where he was to direct the London branch of his now extensive business. His sons Thomas Inger and Henry would manage the Stevengraph Works, which they did successfully for many years after his death.

In September 1888, Thomas underwent throat surgery, for a time he seemed to make a good recovery, but complications set in and he died on 24th October 1888, he was 60 years old. A funeral service was held in London after which he was buried in the family plot in the Coventry Cemetery. The Rev G. Bainton officiated and the coffin was covered in wreaths. The mourners were members of the family and several old friends.

The Stevengraph Works in Cox Street was completely destroyed in the Blitz of November 1940, taking with it the basement area which was said to be full of extra stock. At the time this stock had fallen out of fashion, but today it is collectable worldwide.

As well as Thomas being buried here, there are also his two young daughters, Rose aged 1 year, Alice aged 13 years and his son Henry aged 39, who died in 1899. Also buried here is Annie White, aged 74 who died in 1939. She was one of Thomas's daughters and this is her married name. When the details of Thomas's will were released his estate was valued in excess of £27,000 - quite a large sum of money for 1888.

GRAVE 61 Sq 95.

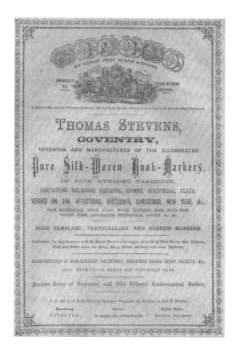

ALBERT SAMUEL TOMSON

Albert Samuel Tomson was born in Radford, Coventry in 1832 and by the age of 12 he had started work at the ribbon weaving business of his father Samuel Tomson.

Albert Samuel Tomson will go down in Coventry's history as the only person to serve in the office of Mayor eight times. This is possibly a record in Coventry, since the election of the first Chief Magistrate in 1345! When first elected in 1881 at the age of 46, he was the youngest holder of this office for a considerable time. He filled the position during Queen Victoria's Jubilee year of 1887, and 10 years later in 1897 for her Diamond Jubilee. He was also Mayor in 1902 for the Coronation of King Edward VII. He also became a JP in 1889.

Whilst Mayor in 1897, in order to celebrate Queen Victoria's Diamond Jubilee, Albert was given permission to present the Queen with examples of Coventry's industrial products. These were two bicycles, a gold watch with a view of the city on its domed case, and a number of exquisite ribbons.

On Thursday 11th October 1883, Albert as Mayor unveiled the statue on Greyfriars Green of Sir Thomas White, a noble benefactor to the city. Also on this day Albert opened to the public, the Swanswell Park and Pool and also Spencer Park in Earlsdon. The weather on the day was not all that it could have been for such an occasion but even so the day's events went well. The streets were decorated with flags, and many shops closed early so that everyone could take part in proceedings. As the Mayor went from one venue to another he was accompanied by city magistrates, members of the council, and distinguished citizens. Spencer Park had been paid for by the generosity of local business man, David Spencer with the sum of £4,000.

An interesting story that is seldom told is that on one occasion when Mayor Tomson was chairing a debate in the Council Chamber of St Mary's Hall a subject on the agenda was road making. The Council wanted to replace the city's cobbled streets with the latest road surface, tarmacadam. Instead of using local contractors it was thought by some that it would be cost effective to purchase the Council's own steam roller. However, some Council members did not want to see money spent on this project and a vote was taken. This resulted in a tie with Albert as Mayor refusing to make the casting vote, leaving the Council finding itself in a deadlock situation.

Albert moved that the issue could be determined over a game of billiards, of all things, in the Mayor's Parlour! The idea was accepted, and representatives from both sides took part. Reported to be an evenly matched game, those in favour of the purchase won the contest. The next Council meeting had the purchase of a steam roller on the agenda, and soon a brand new Aveling Porter was delivered at the cost of £340. It's very doubtful that a dispute could be settled this way in this day and age, where would they start with the paperwork?

Albert died 6th October 1904, aged 72 and was buried with his mother Eliza, his father Samuel Frederick and his brother Samuel James Tomson. Albert's first wife, Elizabeth had died on the 2nd November 1861, aged 30. They had married at St. Mark's Church Birmingham, on the 10th February, 1857. Elizabeth was described as a 'Singing Professor' and was known as Lizzie Stewart. She is buried alongside the Tomson plot, with her parents Mary and William Backhouse. Around edge of the headstone is inscribed:-

> 'And so twill be when I am gone.
> That tuneful peace will still ring on.
> While other bards shall walk these dells,
> And sing thy praise, sweet evening bells.'

After Elizabeth's death, Albert went on to marry Esther, the widow of his next door neighbour. Esther died in August 1889, aged 63. In her obituary it was mentioned how she had 'ably seconded her husband in all offices in which she was possible to assist'.

When Albert's will was read he had left £3000 in a trust fund to provide income to encourage scholarships, entertainment to the students of the Technical Institute, and the School of Art respectively. This trust fund is still in existence today, a lasting tribute to a man who served the city as Mayor and Councillor for so many years. Another lasting tribute to Albert is Tomson Road in the Coundon area of the city. **Grave 4 Sq 58.**

The grave of Albert Tomson, Alongside is the grave of his first wife and her parents. © IW

JOSIAH TURNER

When telling the story of the early days of the cycle industry in Coventry, James Starley naturally features highly. However, Starley would not have considered coming to Coventry had it not been for the suggestion of Josiah Turner. Josiah was a personal friend of John Penn II who employed James as a gardener. Penn had boasted that James had repaired a sewing machine manufactured by Josiah's company. Josiah could not believe this as he thought only his trained engineers were capable of such a task. After some persuasion from Penn, Josiah made the decision to employ James Starley at Newton, Wilson and Co of London, where he was a manager. It was during his time at this firm that Starley made many improvements to the machines. As a result, Josiah provided the necessary funds to enable Starley to take out patents for these improvements.

Josiah backed James Starley in many of his early ideas, having the faith to help see them through to production. With his head for business, Josiah began to think of the best way for them both to move forward in their careers. And so, in the summer of 1861, Josiah persuaded Starley to move to Coventry and helped him set up the Coventry Machinists Company, manufacturing sewing machines. Josiah, who was the manager of the Coventry Machinists Company from the outset, appears to have provided the finances for the business.

As mentioned elsewhere in this book, it was Josiah's nephew, Rowley B Turner, who first introduced Josiah and James to an early form of cycle: an iron-tyred, wooden bone-shaker.

At the time of Josiah's death his obituary stated that he was the former manager the Coventry Machinists Company. Josiah had succumbed to Bright's Disease, which we now know as an inflammation of the kidneys.
Josiah Turner died 17th June 1886, aged 62. **Grave 169 Sq 105.**

JOSEPH WHITE

Joseph White was born in Foleshill Coventry in 1835. At the age of 14, Joseph was indentured to Coventry watchmaker Nathaniel Hill. Previous to that he had worked as a watchmaker's errand boy from the age of 10. His father Thomas had also been a watchmaker in Leicester. At the age of 21, Joseph qualified and he continued to work for Hill for a further two years as a partner in the firm.

In 1860, Joseph set up in business on his own in Mount Street and by 1868 he had purchased Earlsdon House in Earlsdon Street. At the same time he bought 13 artisans houses in nearby Arden Street to accommodate his employees. At this time there were still only about 110 houses in Earlsdon.

Joseph married Catherine Steane, whose brothers George and Isaac ran a well known firm of architects in Coventry, designing Queens Road Baptist Church amongst other buildings. They are both buried nearby. In time Joseph and Catherine were to have 12 surviving children.

The company was named Joseph White Ltd, and later became Joseph White and Son when his eldest son Howard became a director. By the early 1860s Joseph was producing specialised timepieces, components, and precision watches, including deck-watches to be used by the Admiralty, which made its purchases from the best entrants in the Royal Observatory trials at Greenwich. One such time piece served on HMS Waterwitch, HMS Endeavour, and HMS Hermione, and was finally decommissioned on 2nd June 1948. White and Sons were awarded first prize medals for excellence of workmanship and finish in 1867 and 1889.

Joseph supported all his children, and when his son Alfred started a company he was to play a vital role. In 1899, White and Poppe was established and Joseph, who was a wealthy man, guaranteed all its early finances, also becoming a director of the company. By 1907, White & Poppe was the largest British owned manufacturer of proprietary petrol engines, some of which were used in the Morris Oxford of the day, better known as the Bullnose Morris.

When Joseph died in March 1906, he was 71 years of age and he was living at Northwoods House, Frampton Cotterill, Somerset. It was just two years after Catherine had died in November 1904, aged 67.

Joseph and Catherine's son Howard continued to run Joseph White & Son and the business was in operation until the early 1930s when it was taken over by the Coventry Gauge and Tool Company.

Grave 24 Sq 119.

JAMES WHITTEM

James Sibley Whittem was born in 1810, the son of James Whittem, a member of an old Coventry family. His father worked as a currier and it was in this business that James was first employed. A currier is someone who works with leather hides by cleaning and finishing them, also stretching them to a uniform thickness. The hides would then be sent on to be used in shoemaking, glove-making and saddlery.

Young James later opened a business selling agricultural implements, and also bought a run-down farm in Coundon, bringing it up to a high level of cultivation. James was a member of the first committee of The Mechanics Institute and was present at its first meeting in September 1828. James gave much of his time to the institute and in addition to giving lectures; he also donated books, objects for a museum and apparatus for lectures. His friends John Gulson and Charles Bray contributed in the same way.

When a company was formed for the working of Wyken Colliery, James was offered and accepted the position of managing director. Apparently, this company was jointly owned by James and Joseph Paxton, a fact that does not seem to have been common knowledge at the time. He succeeded in making the colliery very profitable for himself and his silent partner. The only real evidence today of the Wyken Colliery is a small spur in the Oxford Canal that is used for mooring of pleasure craft. This was originally where the coal from the colliery would have been loaded on barges to be sent to London.

James built a house for himself called Moat House which overlooked the colliery at Wyken. He lived there for 28 years. Whilst running the colliery, he amassed quite a collection of fossils which had been discovered during the mining process. It was at this time that he was elected as a member of the Foleshill Board of Guardians for the parish of Walsgrave-on-Sowe. He served the parish for many years.

James was a Liberal and in his early speeches he showed he had quite a talent for public speaking. Even at the age of twenty he delivered an accomplished speech at a meeting on Greyfriars Green. James became involved in the repeal of the Corn Laws, which had been established in 1815 as a way of regulating the price of corn. The Corn Laws created a great amount of distress among the working classes in the town, as they were unable to grow their own food, meaning they had to pay high prices to stay alive. By 1839, the Anti-Corn Law League was set up and members of this movement were mainly middle-class manufacturers, bankers, traders and merchants. These people wanted the Corn Laws repealed so that more goods could be sold in Britain and abroad. In 1846, the Corn Laws were repealed by the Prime Minister Sir Robert Peel. In Coventry, Charles Bray and James were two of the people fighting for the repeal of the Corn Laws.

In November 1843, James Whittem was elected as a member of the City Council for Spon Street Ward and on 9th November he was appointed Mayor of Coventry and he held the office for one year. James continued as a member of the Council till November 1846.

James was one of a group of people who were responsible for introducing Joseph Paxton to Coventry in the political sense and championed him to become MP for the city, which he did from 1852 to 1857. This group of people would most certainly have included the likes of John Gulson, Joseph Cash and Charles Bray. Charles Bray was probably a major influence in James's decision making in later life. Bray was well known for his radical ideas as a religious free thinker, and although James was originally a Nonconformist and worshipped at West Orchard Chapel, in the later part of his life he was unconnected to any religious movements or organisations.

James was very interested in helping local people and he established the Coventry Friendly and Provident Institution and acted as treasure for 39 years. The purpose of the institution was to pay its members a financial benefit during times of sickness. It has to be remembered that there was no statutory sick pay in those days.

James died on Monday 9th April 1884, aged 74, having suffered from a heart condition for the previous four years. He died at the Moat House residence, which was at the time said to be at Walsgrave near Coventry. James's wife Ann is also buried in this plot. She died on 18th September 1889, aged 81. **Grave 3 Sq 34.**

WILLIAM WOMBWELL

In the 1800s, the people of Coventry anticipated that a good time was to be had by all when Wombwell's Menagerie visited. It would visit quite often and was very popular as they owned a great variety of animals. In June 1849, Wombwell's had with them a couple of elephants which performed tricks and had brought them a great deal of fame and fortune.

WOMBWELL'S ROYAL MENAGERIE.

THIS superb COLLECTION of ZOOLOGY will remain OPEN during the
COVENTRY FAIR,
IN THEIR USUAL SITUATION ON
GREY FRIARS'-GREEN.
The Collection now contains above
500 **WILD BEASTS, BIRDS,** &c.,
The Productions of all Climates.
THE LION QUEEN
PERFORMS after each Description by the Keeper.
Open at Ten in the Morning, and closes at Ten in the Evening, as the Feeding Time takes place at half-past Nine. Numerous additions have of late been made, constituting the Collection THE FINEST EVER BROUGHT TO COVENTRY.

On this occasion, a procession took place through the town, with one of the Elephants wearing a gilded castle on its back to represent the coat of arms of Coventry. The fair at this time would set up on Greyfriars Green.

On the Sunday afternoon of the fair, William, who was the nephew of George Wombwell, the founder of the menagerie, was sitting with some friends when a disturbance happened amongst the elephants. William went to restore order, but was pinned down by one of the elephants with one of its tusks, and received injuries so severe that he died a few days later on 12th June. He was 25 years of age. Williams's funeral was attended by showmen from all parts of the country, plus thousands of his admirers from Coventry.

The headstone also records the tragic death of Ellen Eliza Bright, who was a performer with Wombwell's Menagerie. She was the daughter of the bandmaster and also a cousin of William Wombwell. She died in January 1850, in Rochester, where the menagerie was appearing. Eliza's performance involved her entering the tiger's cage. Horrifically, on this occasion, she was seized by the throat by a tiger, in full view of the audience amongst whom were her parents. As the audience fled in fear, Ellen fell to the ground, dying shortly after being taken from the cage. She was only 17. Her remains were brought to Coventry and buried in the family grave.

This double fatality caused quite a sensation at the time with two young members of the same family meeting their deaths in dramatic circumstances, only seven months apart.

The headstone is a simple one of slate, and under William's inscription are the words "Wild Beast Proprietor." **Grave 21 Sq 22.**

George Wombwell, William's uncle, died in November of 1850 and is interred at Highgate Cemetery London with a very impressive monument of a life-size sleeping lion.

WALTER WRIGHT

Walter (Watty) Wright was born on 23rd September 1872. His father Joseph was working and living in Iquique, Peru with his wife Margaret at the time and this is where Walter was born. Iquique had developed in the heyday of the saltpetre mining in the Atacama Desert during the 19th century. The city was ceded to Chile after the War of the Pacific from 1879 to 1883 and today Iquique is one of only two free ports of Chile. When Walter was five months old his father died and this left Margaret with the task of returning to Glasgow with four small children.

Walter worked for a firm called Stevenson's Wheel Company of Glasgow who produced wooden wheels described as 'artillery wheels'. In 1906, after becoming managing director, he transferred to premises in Wellington Street Hillfields, Coventry. He brought with him his young family. By 1908, the company had been taken over by another young company, Dunlop, and this was to consolidate their position in the wheel industry.

Walter became manager of Dunlop's newly formed wheel factory. One of Walter's ideas was patented and was described as a "detachable wheel." Today we take the spare wheel of a car for granted but this was the idea for the device described in his patent.

In 1915, Walter travelled to America, to purchase timber for the production of artillery wheels. The only way to cross the Atlantic at this time was by ocean liner. Walter had a first class cabin (number 102 on the promenade deck) of the Cunard vessel R M S Lusitania.

The Lusitania had been launched on Clydeside in 1906 and weighed in at 31,550 tons. Along with her sister ship Mauretania she had held the Blue Riband for the fastest crossing of the Atlantic at various times. Incidentally, White Star Line ordered the building of the Titanic to challenge the supremacy of this pair.

Walter had sent a cablegram to his wife Janet at their Stoke Park home in Coventry to say that he would be returning home on the Lusitania when it left New York's pier 54 on 1st May. Journeys across the Atlantic during the years of the First World War were always going to be dangerous and by Friday 7th May the liner was close to the southern coastline of Ireland. This was the danger area for encountering enemy submarines. The ship's Captain, William Turner, ordered that the lifeboats were swung out, and the bulkhead doors closed as a precaution. Just after 2 o'clock in the afternoon, as passengers finished lunch and with Lusitania 10 to 15 miles off the Old Head of Kinsale to the west of Cork Harbour, a lookout yelled a warning of an approaching torpedo.

Seconds later, there was a huge explosion between the third and fourth funnels, followed by a second almost immediately afterwards. At the time this was thought to be a second torpedo, but it was later established that it came from within the ship. This caused speculation as to whether the ship's cargo was as innocent as the ship's manifest might suggest: there has always been a suspicion that there could have been armaments on board, but this has never been proved. It took just 18 minutes for the Lusitania to sink and of the 1,959 passengers on board 1,198 perished.

Walther Schwieger the Captain of German submarine, U-20 fired the torpedo and the disaster caused enormous political repercussions because amongst those who died one hundred and twenty three were American. This fact alone was enough to ensure that the United States would come into the First World War.

R.M.S. "LUSITANIA"

Walter was 42 when he died. Not many pictures exist of Walter, but poignantly, one was taken on 26th March 1915, on the snow covered shore of Lake Ontario, on the outward journey of the Lusitania. It is reproduced here with the kind permission of Walter's grandchildren Louise and Walter Wright.

Two of Walter's sons eventually worked for the Dunlop. Joe Wright rose through the ranks and ultimately became a member of the Group Board and was awarded the CBE. He retired in 1966. Walter's other son at Dunlop was Jim Wright. He was based at the Suspensions Division and retired in 1970.

Walter's plot in the cemetery is not his grave as his body was never found. The Memorial was placed there in memory of Walter. Buried here though is Walter's wife, Janet who died in 1942, aged 71. Also buried are Walter and Janet's children, twins Walter and Fanny, who both died of measles in May 1909, aged 2 years 4 days apart.

Walter's two sisters are also buried here: Josephine Wright who died in May 1921, aged 57, and Margaret McKim who died in July 1935, aged 75.

On Saturday 9th May 2015, a commemoration was held in honour of Walter, marking 100 years since the sinking of Lusitania. This event was organized by Walter's grandson David in conjunction with the Friends of London Road Cemetery. As well as some of Walter's grandchildren being present also in attendance were great-grandchildren and great-great-grandchildren. Many other relations were present along with members of the Friends of London Road Cemetery, members of the local community and the Lord Mayor of Coventry, Councillor Hazel Noonan. Tributes were made, wreaths were laid, and prayers were said, making it a very moving yet private occasion. **Grave 14 Sq 59.**

Flowers in remembrance of Walter Wright May 9th 2015.   Picture IW

FRANCIS WYLEY

Francis Wyley was educated at Newport school in Shropshire and then studied medicine at Guy's Hospital in London, where he eventually became a Member of the Royal College of Surgeons and a Licentiate of the Society of Apothecaries. He practiced in Coventry for a number of years as a surgeon. Francis then joined the firm of Scott and Wyley in the business of wholesale chemists, and was a senior member of the firm of Wyley and Co.

He was also a member of the City Council for nearly a quarter of a century, and was first elected for Gosford Street Ward in 1847. In 1853, he was one of the chief promoters of the scheme to build a Corn Exchange in Hertford Street, and on 18th August of that year laid the first corner foundation stone. The following year he became secretary of the newly formed Corn Exchange Company.

Francis now bought Charterhouse which was once a Carthusian Priory, and made it the family home. This is possibly one of Coventry's most historic buildings and contains medieval frescos, Tudor decoration, carved beams, and a Victorian extension. In 1859, he was elected as Alderman and in 1860 became Mayor. Francis was twice married, first to Miss Ann Fitzthomas, who died at the age of 26 in 1856. She was the daughter of the Rev. E. H. Fitzthomas. Francis then went on to marry Elizabeth, the daughter of Thomas Sharp, the antiquarian. He was a churchman of a deeply religious nature who also found time to be a trustee of Blue Coat School, and was churchwarden for St Michael's.

Francis died in November 1888, at the age of 78. On the day of his funeral the coffin was placed on the hand drawn bier that belonged to the Cemetery, covered with wreaths and walked in procession from the Charterhouse to the Cemetery, and through the arched entrance tunnel on the London Road. The procession then made its way through the Cemetery to the place of burial.

Francis is interred here with both Ann and Elizabeth. Elizabeth his widow died just four months after Francis in the February of 1889, aged 75.

The son of Francis and Ann was William Fitzthomas Wyley, who was also to become Mayor from 1911 to 1913. He laid the foundation stone for the Coventry Council House on 12th June 1913. William inherited Charterhouse, and when he died in 1940, he bequeathed the building and grounds to the people of Coventry.
Grave 8 Sq 53.

SAMUEL YEOMANS

Born in Coventry on 1ˢᵗ December 1839, Samuel Yeomans entered the watch trade with the company Danziger and Emmanuel. This is where he served an apprenticeship at the end of which he became a freeman of the city.

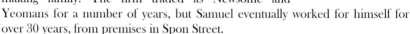

Samuel first went into partnership with Isaac Jabez Theo Newsome, a member of an old Coventry watch-making family. The firm traded as Newsome and Yeomans for a number of years, but Samuel eventually worked for himself for over 30 years, from premises in Spon Street.

Although not a prominent person in public, Samuel was a Liberal and at one time contested Spon Street Ward unsuccessfully. He was also a Freemason, being a member of the Trinity Lodge.

Principally known for his connection with the watch trade, Samuel was for some years Chairman of the Coventry Watch Trade Protection Association. His desire to encourage the industry in Coventry also led him, along with others, to form the Coventry Watch Movement Manufacturing Company. Samuel made a name for himself as a maker of finely finished chronographs, centre seconds, stop watches, as well as ordinary watches in gold and silver.

Samuel died on 18ᵗʰ December 1901, aged 63. His wife, Hannah, died on 2ⁿᵈ January 1896 aged 57. Hannah's maiden name was Welton and there is a headstone in front of this grave which is inscribed with the name Welton, and has a connection to Hannah.

Inscribed round the right hand side of this memorial is this inscription:-

FREDERICK SAMUEL YEOMANS.
KILLED NOVEMBER 14TH 1940.
BURIED IN THE COMMUNAL GRAVE IN THIS CEMETERY.

This wording refers to the fact that Samuel and Hannah's son Frederick was killed during the November Blitz on Coventry during the Second World War. Frederick had also been a watch manufacturer working in Spon Street as his father before him, and also become a Freeman of the city. Frederick's home 8, Palmerston Road was bombed in the air raid, and this is where Frederick died.

During the period of time after the Coventry Blitz, when hundreds of people lost their lives, private burials were forbidden as it would be completely impracticable. As a result, all civilian victims from the raid in November 1940, and from a later raid in April 1941, were buried in a large communal grave in the new, south part of the cemetery. **Grave 6 Sq 44.**

THREE UNMARKED GRAVES WHOSE OCCUPANTS DESERVE A MENTION

Surprisingly, there are in excess of 6,500 monuments in the north section of the Cemetery, the section covered in this book, and when looking across the landscape of the Cemetery, many people make the mistake of thinking that because there are gaps between the headstones, no other graves exist there. This is not the case. Many people would not have had the spare finances for even the most simple of markers, having already spent a considerable amount on the burial plot itself. Over time, a small urn on a grave can be lost and the same can be said for headstones or kerb sets. The nature of the ground in any cemetery can cause even large pieces of stonework to sink below the surface.

In this section I will mention Paddy Gill, Joseph Gutteridge and Benjamin Poole.

PADDY GILL

The first person in an unmarked grave to mention is 'Paddy' Gill, born William Gill in Dublin, 19th April 1820. William came to Coventry at the age of five with his family. Very little is known about William's school days, but he was later apprenticed to a Mr Coleman as a ribbon weaver in Whitefriars Street. This led to him becoming a freeman of the city on completion of his apprenticeship. Even though he was employed in the ribbon industry, William was soon to prove himself in bare-fist fighting, with his first fight taking place on Radford Common on 10th December, 1838. The prize money was five pounds a-side. It was at this time he acquired the ring name of 'Paddy' Gill, taking into account his Irish ancestry. The contest lasted an hour and a quarter, with fifty rounds in total. His opponent, another ribbon weaver, was William Heap. Paddy's pugilistic skills soon attracted backers who were mostly local men with the financial means to put up stake money in the name of what was then classed as sport.

In 1842, Paddy had three victories around the Coventry and Warwickshire area. It should be mentioned at this point, that while prize fighting was hugely popular with the masses, it was illegal and many fights were broken up by the police, only to be recommenced at a later date. Paddy's reputation drew crowds of thousands to some of his biggest fights which were normally staged on quiet heathland to avoid the law. Paddy's appearance was deceiving, standing only five feet five inches tall and weighing just eight and a half stone. This gave him a delicate appearance which often fooled his opponents. He was also known to be a clever two handed fighter. The reputation of Paddy spread country-wide and in June 1845 he fought Young Reed, London's finest on Enshaw Common, Oxford. In the 59th round, Paddy knocked Reed to the floor leaving him unable to carry on. By now prize money for these fights had reached £200. In 1850, Paddy's opponent was Thomas Griffiths of Woolwich. The fight took place on 23rd July, but was to end in tragedy for one of them. This account appeared in the Coventry Standard on the 2nd August of that year:-

'The little village of Frimley near Bagshott, was the scene, on Tuesday, July 23rd, of a prize fight between two men, William Gill and Thomas Griffiths, the former an old professor of the science of pugilism, and the latter an aspirant for pugilistic honours. A special train from London brought down combatants, the seconds etc, besides a numerous company of professors and amateurs of various degrees in Society. The battle money was understood to be £200. The contest, which was a very severe one, was terminated in the 53rd round by a fearful blow, which laid Griffiths insensible on the ground. All means for procuring reanimation were without avail, and he was conveyed to a neighbouring public-house, where he expired between 8 and 9 o'clock in the evening. His antagonist and his associates in the mean time decamped, and have yet eluded the police, who are in pursuit of them.'

The fight with Griffiths lasted nearly two hours and by the end Griffiths was unconscious. One theory was that a second had doped Griffiths using nicotine. Paddy was charged with manslaughter, yet acquitted of the doping charge.

Eventually Paddy retired from the sport and became a publican, along with his wife Mary, becoming the landlord and landlady of the Lamp Tavern in Market Street, Coventry. Paddy seemed to have been making a success of his new career until there was suddenly a deterioration in his mental state, obviously caused by the years of punishment in the ring. Paddy was admitted to Hatton Hospital and sadly this is where he died on 19th October 1869, aged 50. A picture of Paddy hung behind the bar of the Lamp Tavern, showing him in fighting pose with his colours round his waist: 'Coventry Blue' with white spots. The background of the picture showed Coventry's Three Spires and this picture remained behind the bar for many years after Paddy had died, only being removed when the pub was demolished. In the late 1970s in a small book entitled 'More Coventry Cameos' by Eric B. Bramwell, Paddy's grave is described as being surrounded by iron railings and in a dilapidated condition. However now, over thirty years later, there is no evidence at all of a grave marker of any kind. **Grave 36 Sq 116.**

JOSEPH GUTTERIDGE

Joseph Gutteridge has already been mentioned earlier in this book with regards to the book 'Master & Artisan in Victorian England,' which included the diaries of William Andrews and the autobiography of Joseph Gutteridge. Joseph Gutteridge was born in Coventry on 23rd March 1816. His father was also called Joseph and he served in the army, but in 1814, whilst recruiting in Warwickshire, he was taken ill and came to Coventry to be nursed by his wife. He was discharged from the army, after which he became a journeyman in the silk trade. Young Joseph was a delicate child and at the age of five was sent to a dame-school run by Quaker women. On leaving this school, Joseph was put under tuition of a Mr Holland, an itinerant Wesleyan preacher and it was from him that Joseph first found an interest in nature, finding Mr Holland's picture books of animal life a world of wonder that would stay with him the rest of his life. Eventually, Joseph became a pupil at Barker, Billing and Crow's Charity School.

Before his fourteenth birthday, Joseph left school, joining his father in a ribbon factory, learning under him the art of weaving. His hours of attendance in the factory, as with all workers there, were from six am to eight pm in the summer and from eight am to eight of nine pm in the winter months.

Joseph married Sarah on 5th January 1835, at the church of St John the Baptist, Coventry, while still in his apprenticeship. The birth of his first son, however, made things increasingly difficult as Joseph was still an apprentice on low pay. His seven year apprenticeship had passed, but he did not have the finances to pay the stamp duty necessary for completion of the process of becoming a 'freeman'. The family endured great hardship, spending most of their lives struggling against poverty. As the family increased they were beset with other tragedies as their youngest son died and their eldest son was stricken with blindness. Understandably, this put Sarah under great strain and she died in December 1855, of consumption, at the age of 38. Joseph and Sarah had been married twenty years and this was a cruel blow to the struggling family. However, Joseph married again in May 1857, to Mary Hendon. It was not uncommon for someone to marry soon after being widowed, especially with a young family to take care of, while still having to work.

Joseph Gutteridge's biography was first published in 1893 under the title 'Lights and Shadows in the Life of an Artisan' and gives an alternative account of the times to the William Andrews Diaries. Joseph died on 4th September 1899, aged 84. The funeral was a quiet affair, the only people present being a few old friends and neighbours and the bearers being acquaintances from the Hillfields area. Joseph was buried with his first wife Sarah, who, as mentioned earlier, had died young. His second wife Mary is also buried in the same plot having died in 1901, aged 74. **Grave 28 Sq 141.**

BENJAMIN POOLE

Researchers of the Victorian period in Coventry and Warwickshire often turn to three publications written by Benjamin Poole. These are 'The New Historical and Descriptive Guide to Coventry', published in 1847, 'The History of Coventry', published in 1852 and 'Coventry: Its History and Antiquities', published in 1869, sometimes referred to as 'Poole's Coventry'. These very thick volumes are a great source of material for that period of Coventry's history. They contain chapters on architecture and art, myths and stories of Coventry, as well as sections on ancient manuscripts, charters and corporation records. They also contain some fascinating pictures of a Coventry long gone. Some of the buildings in them are still recognisable though, such as the Old Blue Coat School and the Old Grammar School in Hales Street. Also included are some lovely pictures of the Cemetery at the time.

Benjamin was closely connected with the Coventry Standard newspaper for nearly 30 years and in 1858 became the editor, a position he held until shortly before he died. He was also appointed the Registrar of Births and Deaths for the parish of Holy Trinity in 1847, a position he was to hold for 40 years. He was seen as a retiring and sensitive man and not a great deal is written about Benjamin himself but his writings left a legacy that is still used today. Benjamin died on 12th July 1880, aged 80. It seems unusual that this man, who left such a legacy for Coventry, has an unmarked grave. **Grave 155 Sq 117.**

EARLY CREMATIONS

Cremations were still quite a new idea in 1896. They were promoted by the Cremation Society who had built the Woking Crematorium in 1879. At first there were legal objections, but Dr William Price helped establish the legality of cremation. The first cremation at Woking finally took place in 1885, but progress was slow with less than 2000 cremations taking place there between1885 and1900. Today, cremations are very common: in fact, over 70% of funerals are now followed by cremations. The Roman Catholic Church, however, took a stand against cremation, as it was believed that it was a denial of Christian belief in the resurrection of the body. This ruling was not changed until 1963 when, for the first time, cremations were allowed to take place after a Catholic funeral service. While many of the ashes are still interred, the practice of having a person's ashes scattered is also quite common.

JONAS ILLINGWORTH

In November 1896, when Jonas Illingworth was interred in the Cemetery, it was reported in the local press as "a novel burial at Coventry". This was because Jonas was the first person to be cremated and then his ashes interred in Coventry. It was shortly before he died that Jonas expressed a wish that he should be cremated.

The first cremations took place in the country's first purpose built crematorium in Woking, and this is where the body of Jonas was taken by his two sons after his death. The ashes were then brought back to Coventry.

On the day of interment, a glazed urn measuring about 15 inches high and containing the ashes, was placed on a bier and surrounded by many wreaths. The bier was drawn to the chapel by four members of office staff from Leigh Mills, where Jonas had been manager for many years. After the service, conducted by Rev George Bainton, the urn was taken to its final resting place. Wreaths were hung on the walls around the vault and later in the day the vault was bricked up. The vault where the urn was placed is about 3ft deep by 2ft high and is set in the wall that supports the terrace walk. The bricked-up wall was replaced with a pink granite door at a later date.

Jonas was aged 75 when he died and was at that time residing in a house in Hill Street, near Leigh Mills. The ashes of Jonas's brother are also interred here: Rochester Illingworth, who died in April 1909, aged 60. **Grave 1 Sq 47.**

THE CAUSER FAMILY

In the same wall in the cemetery, to the right of Jonas Illingworth, is an identical pink granite door. Behind this door, the ashes of Robert and Georgina Causer were placed. Robert's father Benjamin was a coal dealer with a yard at Coundon Wharf. However, Robert had trained as a watchmaker in Earlsdon, then searching for work had moved to Clerkenwell. This is where he met and married Georgina Tucker in 1890. She was the daughter of an accountant in Islington.

Robert and Georgina moved back to Coventry and lived at 6, Craven Terrace, Craven Street. As time went on and his father grew older, Robert took over the running of the coal business and in the censuses of 1901 and 1911 he is shown as a coal dealer. Robert and Georgina had no children. Sadly, Robert died quite young at the age of 49 on 1st January 1914, and was still living at 6 Craven Terrace. Georgina died 13th May 1933, aged 76 but by this time she was living back in Islington.
Grave 2 Sq 47.

The two niches, Illingworth to the right, Causer to the left.   Picture IW.

RE-INTERMENTS

Re-interments from one graveyard or cemetery to another cemetery are not as unusual as you might think. Here are three such cases in London Road Cemetery: Cow Lane Chapel, West Orchards Chapel, Hill Street and the Conroy Family. These three plots are situated in front of the Nonconformist Chapel.

All three plots where the remains are re-interred are of a regular plot size. Each plot has a headstone, with an inscription detailing where the re-interments are from, but not all the occupants are listed on the stone. Certainly in the case of the chapels, no names are recorded but the records held for each parish will record each individual name. They are not recorded in the Cemetery records.

COW LANE CHAPEL: This was built in 1793 to accommodate a growing congregation, from Jordan Well Chapel, thought to be Coventry's oldest Baptist meeting house which had been built around 1723. The minister, John Butterworth allowed his garden to be used as the site for the chapel, at his Cow Lane residence. The building was galleried with seating for about 800 and the chapel was entered through an archway from the Butterworth's house. Five of John and his wife Ann's children were baptised in the chapel, actually on the days of their birth.

Francis Franklin became a co-pastor in 1799, succeeding John when he died in 1803. Reverend Franklin remained minister until his death in 1852, as mentioned elsewhere in this book. Queens Road Baptist Chapel was built as a replacement for Cow Lane Chapel and opened in 1884. The original house in Cow Lane was demolished in 1948, and the chapel building was converted by the corporation to be used as the reference department of the city library. By 1969 the chapel had also been demolished. It was at this time that all remains including those of Reverend John Butterworth were re-interred at the London Road Cemetery. In 1970, Reverend Hamper conducted a service at the graveside.

WEST ORCHARD CHAPEL: The West Orchard Chapel was situated in Hill Street near the town centre. Many notable people were originally buried here between 1800 and 1971. The Chapel was bombed and destroyed during the Second World War. Interesting to note is that with this re-interment, the re-burial of William Henry Hill in London Road Cemetery means that three mayors from the same family are now buried here: William, his son Charles and his grandson Alick. A small headstone marks the plot of these re-interments.

THE CONROYS: The Conroy family were the subject of a television programme 'Meet the Ancestors' in 2000. In 1999, excavations started in the overflow graveyard for Holy Trinity Church in the town centre. The main purpose of this project was to reveal the remaining walls and foundations of the 13th century Benedictine Priory and the project was called the Phoenix Initiative. The production team of the television programme were invited to film some of the archaeology work. The team discovered the brick lined family vault of the Conroy family. Three members of the family were discovered and the only way that they could identify them was by finding the name plate on one of the coffins. John Conroy was a tea dealer in Cross Cheaping. His wife Sarah died at the early age of 29, in 1827 and was the first to be buried in the vault. It was the name plate from her coffin that was found. From discovering this one name plate historians were able to build a picture of all three people buried in the vault. Also when Sarah's coffin was opened her burial shroud was still in quite good condition and decorated with ribbon. Their daughter Ellen died in 1864 and was buried with her mother, soon to be followed by John in 1870, at the age of 80. Their remains were removed and re-interred at London Road Cemetery. A full burial service took place with the three coffins being carried by members of the team from the television programme and some of the researchers who had worked on the project. This formed the closing scenes for the programme. Marking the plot is a small, black marble headstone.

In conclusion, the term 'final resting place' is not always true. Graveyards and burial places are frequently situated in the way of re-development. With the process of re-interment being treated in a sensitive way, excavations and built works will usually go ahead.

TREES AND WILDLIFE

On entering the cemetery one cannot fail to be amazed by the colours of the trees which come with every changing season. For many people, the autumn is the most stunning time of year, giving a rich palette of colours that even the most casual observer would appreciate.

While the purpose of this book is primarily to tell the stories of people buried in London Road Cemetery, this work would not be complete without a mention of the flora and fauna of the area.

This section, therefore, is concerned with the trees, plants and wildlife found in the cemetery. As mentioned earlier, the trees are an integral part of the design of the cemetery. The intention here is to mention some of the fine specimens that make this possibly one of the best collections within the whole of Coventry. It needs to be emphasised that this is a layman's view and is not in any way intended to be a definitive account.

Joseph Paxton's skills as a plantsman and designer are obvious in the cemetery, and his use of the landscape is a very strong feature. When laying out the cemetery he made full use of the natural contours of the site and in doing so chose plants carefully, to enhance the topography.

Perhaps the best examples of Paxton's clever use of trees are the Candelabra Limes, or Weeping Silver Limes. They are a dominant feature of the cemetery, following many of the curving pathways that weave through the headstones. It is believed that they were first grown in a nursery environment, and then probably planted in their current position in around 1850. Paxton would have chosen these particular trees to create a backdrop to this area of contemplation.

A Candelabra Lime nestling between the headstones.   Picture IW.

Another feature is the Wellingtonia, or Giant Sequoia, a Redwood native to California, which was introduced to this country in 1853. It was named after the first Duke of Wellington and quickly became popular in Victorian landscapes. Other species of Redwood are also present within the cemetery.

The Copper Beech became one of the most widely planted ornamental trees in parks, gardens, churchyards and cemeteries during the 19th century. The most magnificent example in the cemetery is situated in one of the low lying dips in the landscape. Towering above the grave of local historian Abe Jephcott, amongst others, the canopy of this stunning tree measures an impressive 85 foot.

The Copper Beech after a heavy frost 2010.   Picture IW.

The Non-Conformist Chapel is ringed by six Cedars. Originally, there were seven but one was lost a number of years ago, after a heavy snow fall. The Monkey Puzzle Tree, which looks quite lonely to the right of the chapel frontage, was not part of the original planting but was one of a pair either side of the Chapel entrance. Examples of the Cedar of Lebanon can also be found in other areas, with their dramatic shape which adds so much to the landscape.

At the time of writing, a long term conservation programme has been implemented on the trees. Trees that are removed because of disease or being of the wrong type of specimens will be replaced at a later date with specimens that are considered to be in line with Paxton's original planting. This work is long overdue, and will hopefully help to preserve these lovely trees for many years to come.

Wildlife within the cemetery includes the usual suspects: rabbit, squirrel, badger, and fox. However, Muntjac deer have also been spotted. It is thought they make their way along the railway line that separates the two portions of the cemetery.

Butterflies can be seen in the summer months flitting from one self-setting Buddleia to another.

The sound of the green woodpecker can often be heard, together with the songs of other native birds such as robins and blackbirds. Whilst there have been occasional sightings of sparrowhawks, magpies and wagtails are a more common sight, with crows living up to their image sitting ghoulishly atop headstones and monuments!

When you consider the fact that the Cemetery is only 10-15 minutes' walk from the town centre, people are sometimes amazed to find such a diverse selection of trees and wildlife. With the areas around the graves and monuments not often disturbed this makes the Cemetery a perfect habitat for the trees, plants and wildlife to thrive unhindered.

SYMBOLISM WITHIN THE CEMETERY

In any graveyard or cemetery, you will find the headstones and monuments display information regarding the person buried there. Obviously, you would hope to find inscriptions detailing the name, age and date of death, but sometimes you may find certain symbols which may have some relevance to the occupant of the grave, or the circumstances of his or her life or death. In this section I have given a few examples of symbolism you may encounter in London Road Cemetery and the popular meaning behind the symbols.

IHS: this is the most common symbol you may come across in any cemetery. It represents the name Jesus Christ, originally taken from the Greek spelling of his name. Another interpretation is the letters stand for the Latin 'Iesus Hominum Salvator' meaning 'Jesus Saviour of Mankind'. The three letters are sometimes interwoven with each other and often resemble a dollar sign.

A draped urn: this is copied from antiquity as a symbol from classical Greece. It is thought to signify a vessel for the soul and in some cases the ashes of the dead. The draped cloth is also seen as a sign of mourning.

Clasped hands or hands shown in a handshake: this may recall a loving bond, in most cases representing a reunion in the next life of a married couple. It may also represent a farewell to life and welcome to the next.

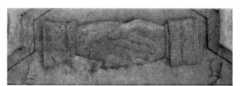

A broken column: this signifies a life cut short, especially the head of the family, but sometimes the death of a young child. Unfortunately, the broken column is often mistakenly thought to be the result of vandalism, or damage occurring due to the age of the monument.

An obelisk: this was a popular choice in the early 19th century when there was a fashion for all things Egyptian. It is also thought obelisks were popular among Protestants who considered the symbol of a cross to be too Catholic.

An anchor: many visitors to cemeteries assume anchors means the deceased was a sailor. This is certainly the case on naval headstones of which there are many within the Cemetery. On other memorials, however, the anchor is used as a Christian symbol denoting hope and salvation. In London Road Cemetery, the best example of an anchor is on the memorial to the Taylor family. The memorial is in two parts. The first part is dedicated to Annette, the only child of Lizzie and George Taylor, who died 2nd October 1886, aged 4 years and 5 months. The later section, added at the front is for Annette's grandmother, Emma Barnacle, who died in 1906, Lizzie, who died in 1907, and George, who died in 1910. The Taylor family were very prominent stonemasons for many years in Coventry and much of their work can be spotted in the Cemetery. The name 'G. Taylor' is normally inscribed at the bottom right-hand corner of any monument produced by this particular stone mason.

A broken flower: this symbol, usually a rose, represents the end of a life. In the Victorian period the rose often adorns the graves of women.

A passion flower: this flower on a grave symbolizes the passion of Christ, the crucifixion and the resurrection. Possibly the best example of this in the Cemetery is on the grave of George Singer.

A hand pointing upwards: this can signify life after death or the hope of a righteous reward in heaven.

A sickle: this can mean the reaping of a life, particularly a young life. An example of this is on the grave of the previously mentioned George Rainbow, the landlord of the Admiral Codrington, who certainly met a particularly early and unfortunate death.

CUTTING'S CORNER

When spending so much time researching people and events in the Cemetery, a lot of time is spent looking through many newspapers, magazines and periodicals of the time. Occasionally something catches your eye: something a little unusual even in terms of events in the Cemetery or matters relating to them. Here are three cuttings: all from the local press. The first makes you think whether such an event would be reported today:-

The Coventry Standard June 1894.

CARRYING COFFINS ALONG THE STREET.

A POINT FOR UNDERTAKERS.

On Monday, at Coventry city petty sessions, before Messrs. Maycock, Hill, and Beamish, Benjamin Bowater, 38 Smithford-street, and Charles Bloor, employed by Mr. Smart, undertaker, 24 Cow-lane, were summoned for causing an obstruction in Earl-street, by carrying a coffin on the footpath.—Mr. Masser defended, and admitted the carrying on the footway, and said that the only question was one of law.—Inspector Walton spoke to seeing the men on a recent evening, and said near Mr. Hayward's shop two passengers had to leave the path to allow the defendants to pass with the coffin. He asked Bowater why he did not get into the road, and he answered, " What? You go on," and the men continued to carry the coffin on the path.—By Mr. Masser: Did not say "That's a nice-looking thing to carry on the footpath."—Mr. Masser contended that there was no case against the defendant, because the information was laid under the Police Clauses Act, and cases decided under that act required the obstruction to be of a cart, carriage, sledge, truck, barrow, or animal. Defendants might have been indicted for an obstruction generally under the Highways Act or indicted for carrying a nuisance. The obstruction of carrying a coffin was no more than that of carrying an umbrella. — The Magistrates' Clerk : Would you say there is no obstruction by carrying a ladder 10 or 12 yards long ? — Mr. Masser: Under the Police Clauses Act, there must be a physical occupation of the soil of the footpath, and this the coffin does not do.—Mr. Maycock: The bench are against you on the point of law.— Mr. Masser: Will you state a case.—The Clerk: The bench would not like to say it is a frivolous application.—Mr. Maycock: Under the advice of the clerk the bench will not grant a case. But this being the first case of the bench they will only order the defendants to pay the expenses, 7s. each. *Standard June 22. 1894*

The second cutting appeared in March 1921 and shows that it is not just pet owners of today who treat their companions like one of the family:-

AMAZING BURIAL.

Coventry Cemetery Scandal.

BULLDOG INTERRED IN CONSECRATED GROUND.

It is probable that few cemeteries throughout the length and breadth of England have been the scenes of a more amazing "interment" than that which occurred at the Coventry Cemetery early this morning, when a pedigree bulldog, in what is believed to have been a solid walnut, brass-studded coffin, was buried with due solemnity in the consecrated portion of the cemetery near the main London road entrance, with the knowledge of the authorities .

A REMARKABLE REQUEST.

It appears that the dog, undoubtedly a beautiful beast, was the treasured possession of a childless couple; the owner is employed in the offices of one of the city's large factories. On Good Friday the owner approached the Coventry Cemetery authorities in great distress, acquainting them of his pet's demise, and requested that he be allowed to bury the dog in the unconsecrated portion of the cemetery.

This extraordinary request was at first refused, as such a burial—antagonistic to all promptings of sentiment—was obviously irregular in the extreme. So touching, however, was the owner's grief, and so strong his dislike to the idea of burying his pet in the back garden, that the authorities eventually gave way, and the burial was consented to, strict secrecy being enjoined.

NOT THE ONLY ONE.

Accordingly, at an early hour this morning, this amazing burial scene was enacted, but not, as might have been anticipated, in the unconsecrated portion of the cemetery, but directly in the consecrated portion not fifty yards from the main entrance. On the right of the centre path leading from the cemetery lodge is a tree-covered mound. In this a grave was dug; the coffin—with the dog's name, "Laddie," in brass studs on the lid—was lowered, and a neat mound marked the spot when a "Midland Daily Telegraph" representative visited the cemetery this morning.

It transpires that "Laddie's" grave is not the only one of its kind in the consecrated portion of Coventry's cemetery, and that similar burials have taken place there previously when canine pets of cemetery employees have died.

IN EXTENUATION?

Councillor T. E. Friswell, Chairman of the Baths and Parks Committee, was interviewed on the subject by a "Midland Daily Telegraph" representative this morning, and his contention was that the proceeding was not "entirely irregular" on account of the fact that other dogs share "Laddie's" resting-place. "Had there not been some dogs there already, we should not have allowed it," said Councillor Friswell. "We thought one more or less would not make any difference."

"We don't want to be inundated with every old maid who has a dead cat or dog," added Councillor Friswell, in explaining his desire to avoid publicity being given to this amazing incident.

In March 1895, this article appeared in the local press, reporting the damage from The 'Hurricane'.

THE HURRICANE.

SERIOUS LOSS OF LIFE.

DISASTERS ON LAND AND SEA.

A gale of exceptional sever raged yesterday, principally in t e South, East, and Midland portions of England, and, as a consequence, a long tale of loss, both of life and property, has to be recorded. Squalls, approaching at times to cyclonic force, prevailed. The havoc among the trees is exceptionally great. Huge trunks in many country districts have been blown to the ground, and in the most violent gusts the branches were broken off in many places, and blown before the wind in a veritable shower.

IN COVENTRY[1] AND NEIGHBOURHOOD.

The gale was at its height in Coventry about one o'clock in the afternoon, and it was at that time most damage was done.

Any visitors going in the direction of the Coventry Cemetery this morning would have been met by numerous individuals bearing away branches, large and small, of trees that had fallen over into the roadway leading to Whitley. And had they entered the Cemetery gate and turned to the right, they would have seen a huge tree uprooted and lying across some outbuildings with its topmost boughs in close proximity to the tower and the windows at the rear of the entrance lodge. The gale must have been terrific hereabouts to uproot so enormous a tree which had in falling

WELL-NIGH DEMOLISHED

two storehouses, including the one that contained the bier carriage. It was between one and half-past that this tree fell, and the damage wi.. be considerable. The fall was preceded by a huge branch from another tree leaving the parent trunk, and this gave a warning to the inmates of the house, which they were not slow to take, to make themselves secure from danger. The kitchen roof was seriously damaged, but under the circumstances the Cemetery Lodge escaped surprisingly well. Near the Church in the grounds a large holly tree was uprooted, and close to the grave of the late Mr. G. Woodcock a huge pine came down, and in its fall demolished a number of smaller trees. Another tree fell across the pathway on the right hand side of the Paxton Memorial, but the damage done in the cemetery appears to have been chiefly confined to that portion near the entrance. At the workhouse the damage done by the gale was not very great, though a large quantity of ridge tiles fell. One circumstance occurred worthy of mention. A single slate was blown from a roof in Whitefriars' Street, and struck and broke a window in the dining hall—a very considerable distance away, as those acquainted with the workhouse buildings will be able to testify—possibly some 50

A picture recording the damage in the Cemetery March 1895, below the same view 2015.

The arched doorway was originally the entrance to a Gentleman's public convenience.

IN CONCLUSION

As I said in the introduction to this book, many of the stories of the people buried in the Cemetery are known to readers who are familiar with the history of Coventry, but some stories are not so well known. I hope these other stories have now come to a wider audience.

Of course, there are a great many people and stories that don't appear here. This is not necessarily because they have been missed of forgotten. Understandably, there are just to many to fit into one book, and a second volume is already planned.

It may also seem that stories concerning women of Coventry buried in the Cemetery have been neglected here. It has been very difficult to find out about the lives of these women, as they were not always recognised for their achievements during the Victorian era.

In addition, sometimes it is obvious that information concerning a particular person may not be the whole story, and more research is needed before being published.

If you think I've missed someone out, an ancestor, perhaps, or someone known to have an interesting story, please feel free to contact me. You may have the missing piece to some of the stories I've come across over the last few years, and your part may help do justice to a story that is part of Coventry's rich social history.

It also seems fitting to note that this book is published in 2015, which is the 150th anniversary of the death of Sir Joseph Paxton, the celebrated designer of Coventry's London Road Cemetery.

Ian Woolley October 2015.

Contact details:-woollian.60@hotmail.com

FURTHER READING

Joseph Paxton, John Anthony.

A Thing in Disguise: The Visionary Life of Joseph Paxton, Kate Colquhoun.

The John Gulson Story, John E. Short.

Coventry: Its History and Antiquities, Benjamin Poole.

The New Historical and Descriptive Guide to Coventry, Benjamin Poole.

The Coventry and Warwickshire Hospital 1838-1948, Desmond Thomas Tugwood.

Wheels Within Wheels: The Story of The Starleys of Coventry, Geoffrey Williamson.

Master & Artisan in Victorian England: The Unpublished Diary of William Andrews. The Autobiography of Joseph Gutteridge, edited by Valerie E Chancellor.

A Harvest of History: The Life and Times of J.B. Shelton M.B.E., M.Rylatt and M. Montes.

Twentieth Century Coventry, Kenneth Richardson.

More Coventry Cameos, Eric Bramwell.

The Silk Pictures of Thomas Stevens, Wilma Sincliar LeVan Baker.

The Vocalists, Lionel Bird.

War Memorial Park, Trevor Harkin.

Many of the above publications are now out of print, but are still a great source for research.

Also extremely useful in the research of this book was the archive at the Herbert, where newspaper articles and The Lowes cuttings collection have proved invaluable.

The Coventry Family History Society has produced a disc that lists all burials and monument inscriptions within the London Road Cemetery, between 1847 and 1972. I strongly recommend people purchase this disc for locating graves of historical interest, or researching your own genealogy.

Pringles, my daily companion around the Cemetery.

Map reproduced courtesy of Coventry Bereavement Services.

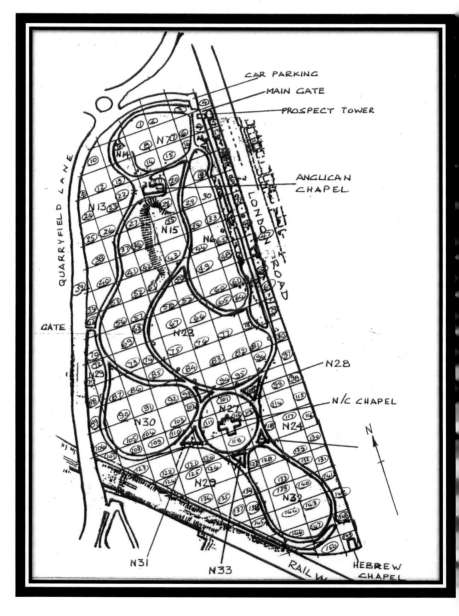